MODEL TRAINS
The Collector's Guide

MODEL TRAINS
The Collector's Guide

CHRIS ELLIS

CHARTWELL
BOOKS, INC.

Published by
Book Sales, Inc.
114 Northfield Avenue
Raritan Center
Edison, N.J. 08818

Produced by
Brompton Books Corp.
15 Sherwood Place
Greenwich, CT 06830

ISBN 0-7858-0221-5

Printed in Slovenia

PAGE 1:
*A very early
Fleischmann 0-4-0
tinplate clockwork
locomotive dating from
the firm's early days as
toymakers around the
turn of the century.*

PAGE 3:
*An English 'piddler', a
simple live steamer of
the late nineteenth
century.*

BELOW:
*One of the best-known
locomotive shapes and
company color schemes
came together on this
Atlas gauge 12 volt DC
electric model of the
1970s – the EMD F9
'covered wagon' in the
Atchison, Topeka and
Santa Fe 'warbonnet'
livery which survives
from the earliest days of
steam traction.*

CONTENTS

INTRODUCTION   6

CHAPTER ONE: The World of Model Trains   8

CHAPTER TWO: The Early Classics   18

CHAPTER THREE: Models for the Masses   34

CHAPTER FOUR: Model Railways Come of Age   50

CHAPTER FIVE: Collecting Today   64

APPENDICES   79

ACKNOWLEDGMENTS   80

Introduction

OPPOSITE, TOP:
A classic home-built layout combining scratch-built, kit-built, and commercial models, all in TT-3 by Allan Sibley.

OPPOSITE, BELOW:
Typical of today's high-quality commercial models is this finely detailed Märklin HO gauge Class C 4-6-2 of the Royal Würtemberg State Railways. The figures are from the Preiser range.

BELOW:
A German toy wooden pull-along floor train dating from c.1880.

The history of model railways goes back even before the first steam train was built, as the pioneering steam engineers built models before they tried the full size engines. Commercially-made models have been available for well over one hundred years and the number of different models produced in that time runs into many thousands in all the leading industrial countries. The three major producers of model railways over the years have been Great Britain, Germany, and the United States, but in recent years Italy and some Far Eastern countries have become more important, too.

All this makes for a complex history of development and improvement, as well as commercial rivalry, with only the two world wars providing breaks in the story. Scales have got smaller and smaller as domestic space has become more restricted. Models and kits have never been better detailed and developed, and never more easily available to anyone who finds model trains attractive. Collectively, model trains are a vast museum of transport in miniature, for not only are contemporary train types always being modeled, but many of the classic historical trains are also recalled with superbly detailed models from all the leading makers.

Model trains began as playthings for children, and though children still appreciate and play with them, the appeal to adults is even greater. Though few would admit it, all but the most toy-like offerings are really toys for grown-ups. Even yesterday's toy trains, the charming old tinplate models of the past, turned out originally for children, are now cherished in the collections of adults. There are hundreds of model railway clubs and numerous model railway magazines supporting what is, in fact, a worldwide interest in scale replicas of trains. The hobby is as close to you as your nearest model railway hobby store, and anyone can join in.

This book tells you what is available, what *was* available, and how to get started. It gives a concise history of the development of the hobby, illustrating many classic models from the past and present. There are hints and tips for starting a collection, collecting themes, and alternative approaches to a hobby that actually has no firm rules.

CHAPTER ONE
The World of Model Trains

BELOW:
This creative layout captures the backwood scene of America at Kahoka Falls and the Eastern Railroad. The HO locomotive is a modified Heisler from a basic Rivarossi model.

The model railway hobby must be one of the greatest constructive and collecting pastimes to have evolved in the modern world. Other hobbies might make rival claims, but in terms of sheer output of product, (train sets, accessories, catalogs, magazines), and the large number of retailers and purchasers over the past hundred years, model railways take some beating.

Almost every small child in the western world has been enchanted at some time, however briefly, by the sight of miniature trains in shop windows, museums, or exhibitions, and until very recent times a train set was considered by many youngsters to be the most desirable Christmas present of all. For very many, and certainly to more than will admit to it, the childhood acquaintance with toy or model trains becomes a lifelong interest: witness the hundreds of adults who visit model railway exhibitions and the countless thousands who belong to model railway clubs and buy model railway magazines. The number of model railway magazines throughout the

BELOW:
This creative layout captures the backwood scene of America at Kahoka Falls and the Eastern Railroad. The HO locomotive is a modified Heisler from a basic Rivarossi model.

world exceeds the totals devoted to other modeling hobbies (such as aircraft, military, and cars); model railway clubs are counted by the score, and in each of the leading model railway countries, (the United States, Great Britain, and Germany) they total several hundred.

Many of those who are interested in model trains as children may not actually follow the hobby into adulthood with an active interest. But with a good proportion of these people the interest lies dormant, sometimes for decades, and in later life they return to it very happily, for railway modeling is a popular retirement activity. Add to this others who use the excuse of their own children to return to the hobby by means of a Christmas train set, and the numbers involved in model railways begins to add up to impressive numbers. These figures have never been properly quantified, but a few years ago in Great Britain a marketing expert

thought that about a quarter of a million people took a very active interest in the hobby and maybe four times that number had a passing interest. In Germany, the leading European country for model railway output, the biggest model railway maker, Märklin, reported sales for 1993 of DM220 million (then about £83 million) and planned a 1994 investment program of DM10 million. Evidence suggests that despite plenty of modern rival hobbies, many of them electronically based, the appeal of model railways is increasing, and this is certainly the case in countries like France and Germany where real railways benefit from a high profile and plenty of investment. By contrast, in some countries where railways are run down or less highly regarded, particularly in Great Britain, the model railway hobby has declined, though the following still remains considerable.

Nostalgia also sustains interest. It is notice-

BELOW:
Typical of today's reasonably priced, well scaled, and accurately detailed commercial models is the Lima HO gauge TGV (Très Grand Vitesse) of the SNCF, the best-known of modern French trains.

able, for example, that in Germany and France where the contemporary railway scene is very exciting and highly promoted, there is a similar keen following for contemporary models. On the other hand, in Britain and to some extent in America, the keenest following is for trains of earlier decades when the home railways were at their most active. In the case of Britain this means that the later days of steam, before railways started to decline, are enormously popular, so numerous 'steam age' models are still produced for collectors. On the other hand, in America, 'first generation' diesel era models (of the 1960s and early 1970s) predominate, again reflecting the greatest interest. In both Great Britain and the United States the greatest numbers of model railway enthusiasts are middle-aged, suggesting that the most popular modeling eras are based on youthful memories of the real railways in their heyday. In mainland Europe, for comparison, many more models produced commercially are of contemporary, or near contemporary, types, reflecting the massive investment that has gone into the European railway systems to produce state-of-the-art trains like the ICE and TGV, as well as slick freight services to compete with road haulage. All this activity is well publicized and very visible to the public. It is no surprise then, that many more children and young adults are still involved in the model railway hobby in the leading countries of mainland Europe.

But whatever the emphasis, there is still massive interest in model railways in every leading industrialized country, and no evidence that it will ever wither. It is worth remarking here that dire predictions of the 'death' of interest in model railways have been made at various times in past century as each new craze has attracted temporary acclaim. In the 1920s it was said that the interest in radio listening would stop model railway activity, in the 1960s, that electric model car racing would replace model railways, and in the 1980s the same was said with regard to electronic computer games. But after each of these crazes has run its course the more traditional model railway hobby has remained as firmly entrenched as ever.

So what is the cause of this continued interest and widespread following? There are several suggested reasons, none of them more dominant than the other. Among them we must include the perennial fascination with all things miniature. We are enchanted by small scale representations of real objects, particularly when they depict all the full-size features with complete accuracy. It is an extra cause of fascination if these miniatures actually work and that is certainly the case with nearly all model railway equipment. The locomotives are mostly powered, rolling stock moves when pushed, and the couplings actually link up. Signals either light up or move, and everything runs on miniature track which is a close representation of the real thing. This complete miniaturisation of both scale and movement must surely be a great attraction and the feature that puts model railways ahead of most other constructive hobbies. A model soldier, for instance, may be completely detailed in every way but he can only stand in a showcase and cannot actually march. Most model cars are similarly static, and even those that race are mostly restricted to a 'slot' in the roadway and this does not replicate the way real cars move along the road.

In addition to this most of us can relate to model trains quite easily – nearly everyone travels on real trains at some time or other. When that happens there is all the exciting atmosphere of the station and the movement

of trains and equipment to add an extra dimension to the very notion of rail travel. This excitement is reflected in contact with or possession of the models, particularly if they are models of trains we have traveled in or seen. And, naturally, the sheer power of the locomotive is reflected in a model of it. Locomotive power is impressive, and in a steam locomotive, there is the added bonus that it is all made visible by means of the wheel movement and the exhaust. This is nicely simulated on a model, and anyone, for example, who has seen the real *Flying Scotsman* locomotive in action, a symphony of steam, sound, and graceful movement, will have no difficulty at all in relating to a scaled model of the same locomotive. While this is an obvious example, it makes the point that model railways easily capture the imagination, more so perhaps than most other models, by virtue as much as anything of the drama, variety, and excitement of real railways.

Not unique to model railways, but instrumental in turning it into a collecting hobby, is its vast scope. Historic or modern? Steam, diesel or electric? Real railways are always

LEFT:
A Union Pacific GP7, altered and detailed from an Athearn HO model.

BELOW LEFT:
The impressive Southern Pacific 'Cab Forward' Class AC4 4-8-8-2 produced as a limited-edition brass model and running on John Porter's HO American layout.

BELOW:
An interesting line-up of American HO motive power on Clive Tate's atmospheric Kahoka Falls layout.

RIGHT:
A superb scratch-built North Eastern Railway 4-4-2 Atlantic O gauge.

BELOW:
A fine-quality gauge O old time tank wagon of the Deutsche Reichsbahn made by the German firm of Micro Metakit.

evolving with new designs of locomotives and equipment continually appearing. There is never any shortage, therefore, of inspiration for the model manufacturers and kit makers. Even if designs don't change, the liveries and markings do, all reflecting onward progress and change in miniature. Added to that, the selection of past types for reproduction, means that hundreds of new models are produced each year. Then the real railways had (and still have) vast ranges of equipment themselves for manufacturers to reproduce in miniature. So having made one class of locomotive or passenger car, for example, the model manufacturer will follow it up with another, and so on. Enthusiasts face an overwhelming choice of trains and accessories from every era and region of railway history.

Thick catalogs are published annually by the big manufacturers showing current production, and as old models are dropped from a range and new ones are added, there is a constant turnover of available models from manufacturers' 'back lists', as well. Older ones become rare and sought-after, and even the old catalogs themselves become desirable items to collect and keep. Allied to this is the price range of the kits and models. There really is something for every pocket. Because of the enormous range of different models available at any one time, plus a large second-hand market, models are obtainable literally at pocket money prices at the lower end of the scale, ranging up to expensive models which cost four or five figures in any currency at the top of the range. Bespoke made-to-order

models, also available from specialist suppliers or individual craftsmen, might be more expensive still. But as a collection can be built up piece by piece, the model railway hobby suits every level of expenditure. And it is a hobby that can last a lifetime if you wish. Even if there are periods where for some reason you suspend active model making or collecting, you can still keep in touch with the hobby by reading the model railway magazines and visiting the many model railway hobby shows. Finally, as it is possible to build your own models by hand from raw materials and component parts (such as wheels), it is possible to get involved and yet spend very little.

Scales and gauges

Before proceeding to look in more detail at what is available to collectors, it is necessary to say something about scales and gauges. Those already familiar with model trains will know about this already, but anybody new to the subject may be mystified by such refer-

ences as O gauge or 1:87 scale. To keep a lengthy subject short it is helpful to say that all model replicas are usually described by scale. Thus a 1:12 scale replica of anything is 12 times smaller than the original. Model trains are described like this, but there is a further complication with trains in that the track gauge is also needed if the description is to have full meaning. Track gauge is the distance between the running rails. What is known as standard gauge is the old British measurement of 4ft 8½in., now more commonly expressed in metric terms as 1435mm in Europe. Anything wider than this is called broad gauge (example Spain, 5ft 3in.-1674mm), and anything narrower is called narrow gauge (typically 1000mm or 750mm).

For technical reasons caused by the limitations of scale reduction, the track gauge of the model does not always reduce strictly to scale. The most notorious example of this is British OO gauge. A 1:76 scale reduction of the model gives a measurement of 4mm to one foot. This

BELOW:
A contrast in scales and gauges; a German 0-6-0T reproduced by Märklin in three different sizes. From top to bottom: Gauge 1, HO gauge and Z gauge.

means the track gauge reduced to scale would be 18.83mm, but OO gauge is actually 16.5mm, rather under width for the scale. This sort of thing introduces further complexity into the hobby, but nothing that cannot be overcome.

The common scales and gauges now encountered are as follows:

Gauge	Scale reduction	Track gauge(width)	Variation
G	1:22.5	45mm	Can also depict 1:24, etc

This is a large-scale narrow gauge size whereby the 45mm gauge can depict either 750mm or 1000mm full-size gauge and the model scale varies accordingly.

1	1:32	45mm(standard gauge)	1:30
O	1:45	32mm (standard gauge)	1:48(USA), 1:43(UK)
S	1:64	⅝inch (16.5mm)	
P4/S4	1:76	18.83mm	
EM	1:76	18.2mm	
OO	1:76	16.5mm	

The above three gauges are all to the same scale, but EM and P4/S4 evolved in attempts by enthusiasts to correct the inaccurate under-width track gauge of OO. Only OO is supplied by the main manufacturers. EM and P4/S4 conversion has to be done by the modeler or by specialist firms.

HO	1:87	16.5mm	1:80(Japan)

The HO gauge, 1:87 scale is the world standard and dominates the model railway hobby with a following of around 80% of all modelers. In Britain only, OO gauge to a slightly larger scale is the trade equivalent.

TT	1:120	12mm	
TT3	1:100	12mm	14.2mm track gauge

TT3 is the British equivalent to TT with the same scale/gauge disparity as for OO and HO. Some enthusiasts have corrected the British gauge to true scale width of 14.2mm.

N	1:160	9mm	1:148 scale(UK) 1:150 scale(Japan)

After HO, N gauge has the greatest following and there is very large trade support. British and Japanese models are to a slightly larger scale than all others. There is a British fine scale equivalent of 2mm to 1ft, 1:152 scale, 9.5mm gauge, sometimes called OOO gauge.

Z	1:220	6.5mm	

Narrow gauge models are variously described. While the scales are the same as for the standard gauges listed above, all the models run on narrower gauge track. The most popular are as follows: HOe(depicts 600-750mm gauge), HOm (depicts metre gauge), Oe, Om, Nm, 1m. Some British and American narrow gauge models are differently described. Most common are: 009(1:76 scale on 2ft 3in. gauge), On16.5 (depicts 2ft 3in./2ft 6in. gauge), Sn3 (3ft gauge), etc. There is also a very large scale, generally called 16mm scale running on 32mm gauge track. Some early models were to much larger gauges, such as 2 and 3.

Terminology

The following are terms commonly encountered in descriptions of model trains.

Tinplate: The description given to early models (mostly pre-1960) which were most frequently made largely of printed or enamelled tinplate. However, some tinplate models are still made today.

Coarse scale: Earlier models had rather liberal wheel and track sizes. Though the gauges were standardized, wheels tended to be thick, flanges deep, and rail cross-sections high, all well beyond strict scale dimensions.

Fine scale: More recent models may have wheels (and matching track) made very close to true scale dimensions and cross sections. This is known as being made to fine scale standards.

It should be noted that most models these days are made with wheel and track standards which are not fine scale but are of visually acceptable appearance commensurate with manufacturing limitations and the need for young modelers to be able to handle them. Most modern mass-produced models are made to this sort of standard with wheels and track of scale appearance even if they are,

strictly speaking, beefed up rather over scale.

Two-rail, three-rail, stud contact: These are common descriptions, mostly self-explanatory, for the electrical system used for model propulsion. Early electric models were most often three-rail (there was a third conducting rail between the running rails). Stud contact replaced the rail with studs on the sleepers which the locomotive pick-up bridges. Most modern models (Märklin is an exception with HO stud contact) now use two-rail which is more realistic, all power passing through the running rails. Most three-rail and stud systems use alternating current (AC) and two-rail systems use direct current (DC), usually 12 volts. However, some systems, such as Märklin gauge 1, are AC on two-rail track.

Command control: The modern control system using micro-processors and electronic technology and memory for controlling locomotives and operating systems. Locomotives have to be fitted with suitable modules.

Ready-to-run or off-the-shelf: Terms usually used to describe mass-produced models of locomotives, stock, and accessories available from model shops, as opposed to kit-built or scratch-built, or hand-made models.

BELOW:
Typical of the early years before gauges were fully standardized is this tinplate Bing toy train in Midland Railway colors, produced for the British market in an unusual 28mm gauge, c. 1900.

LEFT:
Modern HO models are highly-detailed and extremely realistic in properly modeled settings, such as this Märklin model of the veteran DB Class 191 electric loco in a wintry station platform.

BELOW:
A very fine and much sought-after OO gauge model by Tri-ang (later released by Hornby too), the attractive and well-scaled Great Western Lord of the Isles, a 4-4-2 'single wheeler', and one of the classic British locomotives.

CHAPTER TWO
The Early Classics

Model railways of sorts have existed as long as real railways, for miniature representations as pull-along wooden nursery toys or cheap lead playthings were produced in the 1830s in the days when the first steam railways opened, and such toys continued to be made throughout the nineteenth century. But model railways actually pre-dated the appearance of the real thing. Probably the first one appeared as long ago as 1784, built by William Murdoch.

RIGHT:
Possibly one of the first model steam engines ever built, Trevithick's model was constructed in the closing years of the eighteenth century to demonstrate his scientific theories.

Murdoch was a pump maker employed by Boulton & Watt, the firm of the steam pioneer James Watt. While Watt had briefly considered adapting his steam engine design for propelling boats and carriages, he preferred to concentrate on building stationary engines for pumping and machinery use, for which there was big demand. Murdoch made a model of a vertical boiler locomotive to show his employers what could be done, but they told him to forget such ideas and get on with pump making.

Murdoch was based in Cornwall installing pumps in tin mines and here he met the engineer Richard Trevithick, son of a tin mine manager and an engineer concerned with mine engines. Whether or not Murdoch influenced Trevithick is not known, but Trevithick also had ideas for harnessing steam to the haulage of wagons on the then horse-drawn wagonways that were already well established in the mining industry. To put over his ideas to the mining interests Trevithick also made models between 1797 and 1798, and he instantly improved on Murdoch's ideas by using a horizontal boiler to allow higher steam pressure, a principle that has been used ever since in steam locomotives. A vertical

This is a charming replica of Timothy Hackworth's Royal George, *built in this form in 1827 for service on the Stockton & Darlington Railway.*

associate engineer, Timothy Hackworth, improved again on Trevithick's ideas by connecting the driving wheels to increase traction, and they also introduced the first use of the bogie, or truck, to improve flexibility of running, all this being done on the Wylam railway. The biggest impact, however, was made by George Stephenson, whose first locomotive, *Blucher* was built for a colliery line in 1814; he realized the importance of adhesion and adopted the flanged wheel on edge rails, the principle that has been used to this day. Stephenson also engineered and provided the first locomotive (*Locomotion*) for the celebrated Stockton & Darlington Railway which opened on 27 September 1825, the world's first practical commercial railway which carried both passengers and freight over a 26 mile route. The success of this line led to many proposals for other steam railways. Stephenson, with his *Rocket*, won the Rainhill trials, held at Liverpool in 1829, in a contest to provide the power for the even more ambitious Liverpool & Manchester Railway. *Rocket* became the most famous of all early locomotives, the one everyone has heard of, and numerous models in various scales have appeared over the years.

Stephenson's fame was such that he engineered the first German railway from Nuremburg to Fürth in 1835, and also built the first German locomotive, *Adler*. Stephenson's early influence was considerable. He established the standard gauge of 4ft 8½in. largely because it was the width apart of the wheels of horse-drawn carts. The pioneer French steam engineer, Marc Sequin was inspired by an early visit to the Stockton & Darlington Railway to better Stephenson's ideas, and *Saxonia*, the first locomotive in Saxony (Leipzig–Alten, 1837) was built to a Stephenson design.

Models of all these early locomotives (and some of the rolling stock) have been made in various scales in recent years, and a collection of pioneer railway models, or, indeed, a layout based on the earliest days would have a great attraction. *Adler* and *Rocket* are the most frequently produced models, appearing in nearly every scale. A rare acquisition would be one of the brass live steam O gauge models of *Locomotion* made in the late 1980s as a limited run by a small German specialist model builder.

Much sought after by established collectors are, of course, genuinely old models from the earliest days. These are extremely rare and

cylinder with a piston drove the wheels, and a large flywheel ensured smooth motion.

We know all this because one of Trevithick's original models of this period survives in the Science Museum, London; it is probably the world's oldest model steam locomotive (to 4½inch gauge) and is obviously valued beyond price. Trevithick built his first actual full-size steam vehicle in 1801, a road carriage which caught fire and was burnt out in early trials. A second steam road carriage in 1803 did not excite commercial interest, though it was demonstrated in London, but in 1804 Trevithick built his first locomotive to run on rails in the way postulated by his demonstration models. This first engine was for an ironworks at Dowlais, Merthyr Tydfil, Wales, and made its first run on 21 February 1804, opening the age of steam railways. In 1805 a second engine of the type was built for the Wylam colliery at Gateshead where it actually ran on the wooden tracks of the old horse-drawn wagonway. A modern plastic kit of this first practical locomotive type was made by Airfix some years ago and it is still obtainable.

Steam locomotion was initially slow to catch on, but notable work was done by John Blenkinsop who developed Trevithick's ideas to provide rack-and-pinion steam traction for the Middleton Railway of 1812, a line that still exists and is probably the oldest surviving railway from steam days. William Hedley and an

LEFT:
A very early commercial model made by Radiquet of Paris, c.1885 and possibly sold in Britain by one of the first model railway suppliers, Stevens Model Dockyard. The wheel arrangement of 2-2-2 is typical of many real locomotives of the mid-nineteenth century.

BELOW:
One of the more elaborate 'Piddler' or 'Dribbler' models of the late nineteenth century, this particular model, Pilot, *is thought to be of English or Irish origin.*

Two early O gauge clockwork locomotives by Charles Rossignol of France, dating from the end of the nineteenth century. Delightfully quaint, these clockwork models still run well.

most are in museum collections. The first working live steam model locomotive with track and wagons is said to have been made in Spain in the 1850s, and the earliest recorded toy (non-working) locomotive dates back to 1826, made by a Nuremburg toy maker, Matthias Hess. The Prince Imperial of France had a toy railway layout in 1860. The earliest recorded clockwork model locomotive dates from 1867, made in London. By the 1860s miniature working steam engines were being manufactured and offered for sale in Britain, France, and Germany. Most of these models were in brass, had simple oscillating steam engines, were spirit fired, and usually had four wheels. They ran on brass track or even on no track at all. Because they left a stream of water and oil behind them from their simple boilers and cylinders, they were universally known as 'Dribblers' or 'Piddlers', and many a domestic carpet was spoilt when the new model was set up and run indoors for the first time. Later 'Dribblers' had more wheels (typically six) and other features like cabs and dummy domes, but the simplest and earliest models looked like miniature Stephenson locomotives. They were quite large models, typically of 2½ or 3½ in. gauge (64mm or

89mm), though there were some smaller versions. Because they were made in such large numbers, Dribblers do turn up from time to time at auctions or even in antique shops, but invariably the price is high. However, the chance of acquiring one of these charming relics of early model railway history is certainly possible for any collector who can afford it. Wooden pull-along or even card cut-out or cheap tin outline models from the mid-nineteenth century also appear and are certainly worth looking for even if they are not commonly seen or offered for sale.

Model railway development advanced considerably during the 1870s. The leading British maker was Stevens Model Dockyard, but the center of activity was in Nuremburg which was (and still is) the home of the German toy and model industry. Tinplate printing and fabrication combined with clockwork mechanisms to make a much cheaper toy than the brass 'Dribbler'. Even cheaper were smaller, unpowered pull-along toy trains, also made in tinplate. The leading early maker was the firm of Schoenner, founded in 1875. In the 1880s another maker, Georges Carette, also Nuremburg-based, came to prominence. Scales and gauges in these early days were haphazard, to say the least, with models made to any convenient size and with the gauge not always matching the scale. The early models did not particularly resemble any particular types either, being mostly of generic appearance. There was similar activity in the United States, and most of the early toy trains in America were centered in New England. Beggs, Bergmann, Garlick, and Brown were early makers, mostly in tinplate and variously with clockwork and steam propulsion. Most of the early models were produced for floor running, not to run on track. Some French tinplate models were also made at this time. Two firms, Dessin and Maltète et Parent made some of the best looking clockwork and pull-along trains of the 1880s, capturing the true character of contemporary railways, even though the models were floor runners rather than rail runners.

An odd form of propulsion used by some toy makers in these early years was a flywheel drive whereby a string was wrapped round the axle, which carried a heavy flywheel. When the string was pulled sharply away, sufficient momentum was imparted to the model to carry it across the floor. Crude as it was, this

ABOVE:
A rack locomotive and coach with mountain scenic effect, signal box, and signs, all in tinplate, for gauge O, made between 1895-1900 by Märklin.

LEFT:
Early models by Märklin. In the background is a signal, and 'Central' station, with provision for interior illumination by two candles. In the center is a 0-4-0 clockwork locomotive of about 1900 with a four-wheel carriage. In the foreground is another clockwork 0-4-0, dating from about 1910 and sold by the London store, Gamages.

23

entertaining mode of playing trains lingered well into the twentieth century. A further development of the early years was the use of cast iron instead of tinplate for the toy trains sold in America. This seems to have been adopted first by American manufacturers, but as a result German and British makers exporting to the United States also used this material.

The most significant development took place in 1892 when the firm of Märklin entered the model railway field. Theodor Märklin had been producing tinplate toys since 1859, mainly doll house accessories. His son, Eugen, expanded the business by taking over a much larger tinplate toy company in 1891, and moving all its equipment, as well as the workforce, to his home town of Göppingen. By this time real railways had entered a golden era of technical development and expansion and had become the dominant form of land transport. Many small firms were producing toy trains and it was clearly an opportune time to make an impact. Märklin, with

their newly-acquired tinplate printing plant, caused a stir at the Leipzig Spring Fair of 1892 with the unveiling of a clockwork toy train that came in set form with a sectional track system that had a geometry allowing it to be made up piece by piece into a layout of any size. This was a major breakthrough, which instituted the idea of train sets, accessories, and track available in a co-ordinated range, with related models, and has been the way of making miniature trains ever since.

With these models Märklin also introduced the idea of constant scale and gauge right through the range. These first models had a track gauge of 45mm and Märklin called this 'No 1 gauge', logically enough. The early models were caricature trains by today's standards, the first locomotives, for example, having a 'single wheeler' chassis with just one driving wheel each side and a small trailing wheel. When larger models were made with track gauges of 2in. and 2½in. (50mm and 64mm), they were designated No 2 and No 3 gauges (sometimes written as II and III), and

BELOW:
Steam tram locomotives and tram (street car) trailers with passengers and station for gauge III produced by Märklin in tinplate, c.1897.

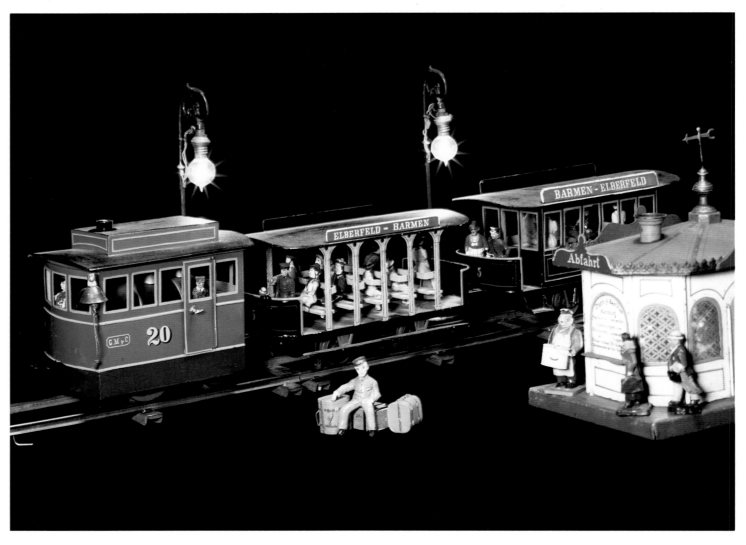

ABOVE:
Made by Carette for Bassett-Lowke in gauge 2, this Great Western Railway full-brake clerestory coach dates from before World War I.

in 1895 when a range of smaller models was introduced, with a 32mm track gauge, it was designated 'No O gauge'. For many years, in fact until the 1920s, O gauge was the smallest commercial scale and it was considered very compact. Gauge 1 was the most favored scale well into the 1900s and the greatest number of models were made for this gauge. This worked out at 1:32 scale, though some of the early models were rather liberally interpreted in size. Märklin's new models were well received and the company expanded rapidly. In 1895 it moved to a vast new factory, and in the next few years model trains formed a constantly expanding segment of their toy output, eventually becoming the major activity of the company. Over 100 years later Märklin are still going strong; they dominate the model railway industry in Germany (and have flourishing export sales, too), and are considered the world's 'senior' model railway company.

Other manufacturers saw the logic of Märklin's ideas, and soon all other makers were standardizing, too, for the most part adhering to the same range of scales and gauges as Märklin. Clearly 1892 was the watershed year for model railways when all the key ideas that hold good to this day took shape. The standardization of model railway scales was also the starting point for a famous British company, Britains, another firm which is still thriving

over a hundred years later. Britains were never model railway makers, but they saw that accessories would be needed and started making model farm animals, station and railway figures, and platform fittings (ticket machines, seats, etc). Everything matched Märklin's 1:32 scale. The first models, released in 1894, were pleasingly realistic lead figures for which the company acquired a good reputation. When the Boer War started in South Africa in 1899, Britains diversified into model soldiers and continue to produce them today. Britains' railway figures were probably the first top class model railway accessories, though many other makers, including Märklin themselves, were soon producing them. Today, there are many more model railway accessory makers than there are train set makers.

The last five years of the nineteenth century saw other German firms join in the business that Märklin had created. Schoenner and Carette were already in the trade and they went up-market, producing models rather superior to Märklin's. Bing was another toy maker which switched to railways in the wake of Märklin's example and soon became Märklin's greatest competitor. Plank, Falk, Issaymeyer, and Bub were other companies whose products were well-known, though most of these firms produced cheaper or cruder

miniatures. Though Bub became a very large company, for example, it was never considered a competitor by Märklin. All these firms were in or near Nuremburg making the city truly the 'model railway capital' of the world at the time. Interestingly, though there are fewer big firms producing model trains today, there are still a fair number in the Nuremburg area and it probably still claims the world's greatest concentration of model railway firms in any one area.

Most of the output in the 1895-1900 period was still very toy-like and although the models had charm and durability, very few of them were representations of actual locomotive or rolling stock types. This all changed from about 1900, and the impetus came largely from Great Britain. In the closing years of the old century, the leading British firm of Stevens Model Dockyard were making more realistic models than most others, in that company names and markings were being applied even though the model engines themselves were nondescript. A key figure in the development of model railways was W. J. Bassett-Lowke, a young model engineering enthusiast who had set up his own small business in Northampton, England, in 1897. Bas-

sett-Lowke found the supply of castings and parts for models hard to come by (Stevens and Clyde Model Dockyards were the only model firms of any consequence in Britain), so he started to make his own parts, to sell to other enthusiasts. The founding of the magazine *Model Engineer*, by Percival Marshall in 1898, gave a boost to Bassett-Lowke's company, as he started a mail order business through the magazine. Bassett-Lowke was only selling parts like wheels and boilers for amateur constructors, but an importer of German toys advised him to visit the Paris Exhibition of 1900 where leading German toy makers would be exhibiting. In Paris Bassett-Lowke was highly impressed with the quality of the miniature trains by Bing and Carette, who were now producing some good-looking models of German locomotives. Bassett-Lowke realized that nobody in Britain could achieve the quality of manufacture and finish that Bing and Carette were displaying. He sought out Stefan Bing, head of Bing Werke (who subsequently became a lifelong friend) and asked if Bing could make models of British locomotives of similar quality. A deal was agreed, and it was found that one of Bing's German-style 4-4-0 gauge 3 locomotives

could be adapted with a new body to depict the *Black Prince* of the London North Western Railway company, then the most prestigous rail company in Great Britain. The first models arrived for sale under the Bassett-Lowke label in 1902 and made the company's name. Bassett-Lowke enlisted the aid of another keen model engineer and draughtsman, Henry Greenly, to design further models for Bing to manufacture specifically for the British market. Similar deals were made with Carette, and to a lesser extent with Märklin and Schoenner.

Over the next few years, until the outbreak of World War 1 in 1914, a profusion of models in all gauges, live steam, clockwork, and later electric, flowed from these German companies into Britain. The top-of-the-range models were remarkably good representations of actual types, though there was still a good proportion of more nondescript 0-4-0 tank engines, for example, at the bottom of the range, finished in various company colors but not representative of any actual engine types. For the British market some of these cheaper models were the same as those sold in Germany but with British company names and colors instead.

Coaches and rolling stock for the British market were also made by the German firms, though Bassett-Lowke set up their own production lines in Britain for rolling stock and locomotives, some of them in kit form. Most of the classic British locomotives of the day were made for Bassett-Lowke in Germany, but other companies in Britain also latched on to the same idea. Most famous of all was the British department store Gamages who had Bing and Märklin make models for them (different again from those supplied to Bassett-Lowke) to sell under the Gamages trade name, and in addition to this, further Bing and Märklin British-style models were imported by other smaller distributors. This saw the beginnings of the tendency for the general market to apply bogus or incorrect markings to a model in order to widen its appeal. An early example was the very popular *King George V*, another LNWR 4-4-0, produced in great numbers as a model. It appeared in correct LNWR finish, but versions were also produced in Midland Railway, Great Western Railway, and Great Northern Railway finishes, all of which were bogus.

Schoenner made even more 'de luxe' models for Bassett-Lowke including some

ABOVE:
One of the very early models built for Bassett-Lowke by a German supplier, this London & South Western Railway bogie express locomotive dates from 1903-04.

superb 3-in. gauge live steam 4-4-0s. This larger gauge was called 'gauge 4' and is rarely encountered today. The British insistence on better scale appearance for the top models rubbed off on the German manufacturers, for they also made more accurate-looking models for the domestic market. Märklin, Bing, Schoenner, and Carette also made models for the American, Swiss, and French markets, though the size of the British market (and the British Empire of those days) seems to have ensured that the export market for British-style models was the biggest, and there was certainly a profusion of types in all scales from gauge O upwards.

The American contribution to the early days of model railways was the first use of electric traction; one of the earliest references to electric model railways was in 1900 from the Carlisle & Finch company of Cincinnati. They advertised a model tram set in gauge 2 which took its power from an ordinary 6 volt wet-cell accumulator. This first electric train set, with its 6 volts DC running and two-rail electrification, contradicts the popular notion that two-rail DC is a post-World War 2 development. Carlisle & Finch made other primitive electric sets including a mine loco-

motive and dumper cars, and eventually they made some more ambitious locomotives and trains, all electric. Another American company which developed a very comprehensive two-rail 6 volt DC range was Voltamp who were also one of the earliest companies, possibly the first, to develop an automatic coupler that joined up when two vehicles were pushed together. Voltamp also had automatic reversing and working headlamps, all features taken for granted today, but introduced by them in the early 1900s. A further American company offering an electric range was Knapp.

Märklin's own history states that their first electric trains appeared in 1897, but most authorities give 1904 as the date when electric Märklin trains were available in any quantity. Whatever the case, the Europeans favored high voltage (40-60V) motors with three-rail track, using the center rail as a common return. Power was most often taken from the domestic light sockets with a wiring system that looks distinctly hazardous to modern eyes. Light bulbs were fitted to the controler to provide resistance in the earliest Märklin power units. Bing produced their first electric models in 1908, but generally speaking, electric traction was slow to spread in Europe before World War 1, largely due to differing electrical arrangements in individual countries. The high voltage German system, for example, was frowned upon in Britain. Many of the earliest models fitted for electric traction were, logically enough, models of electric locomotives and the early 'steeple cab' type of locomotive was widely produced in miniature by all the leading makers, as were some early underground trains and trams.

The model railway industry grew quite extensively in America in the 1900s, with some famous names having their roots in these years. Ives had been among the first of the New England toy train makers in the 1870s and 1880s, but by 1900 they were producing a range of clockwork floor running trains. In 1901 they introduced their first train sets with track, these being O gauge clockwork, and the first home produced O gauge models in the United States. In 1904 they introduced a gauge 1 clockwork range, again the first American maker to do so. In 1910 they added electric O gauge (with a center third rail) to their output and in 1912 they moved into an electric version of their gauge 1 range. Like Märklin in Germany, they also went heavily

into accessory production with a large selection of structures and figures to supplement the train sets. These accessories were mostly tinplate but most of their locomotives had cast iron bodies. Lionel was another famous name who started about 1902 with large two-rail electric trains at 2⅞in. (74mm) gauge. By 1903 they had moved into smaller models with a unique gauge of 2⅛in. (53mm) which they used for many years. This became known as 'Standard' gauge. Trams and steam locomotives were the first electric models they made in this gauge. In 1910 they made some good models of electric locomotives, and in 1915 they first produced a gauge O range in center third rail electric, the gauge they have stayed with until the present day. The Haffner toy company commissioned in 1907 a Chicago hardware maker called Metzel, to make some clockwork trains which were so successful that Metzel marketed the trains themselves under the name American Flyer. Haffner later carried on by themselves making toy train sets, mostly to O gauge.

Interest in model trains grew in the early 1900s, fueled by the ever-increasing selection of models over a wide price range. Though toy trains had always been regarded as playthings

BELOW:
The West Coast Joint Stock 12-wheeled saloon sold by the Caledonian Railway in 1909-10 to advertise the West Coast route from England to Scotland. It was made by Carette of Germany to the specification of Bassett-Lowke. Though nominally to gauge O, these models were really decorative floor runners.

RIGHT:
A magnificent collection of early models by Märklin which shows the charm of tinplate toy trains to perfection. Top right is a PLM (French) Pacific in clockwork, produced in the 1914-25 period. In the engine shed is a German Pacific of 1937, and the others are models of the 1920s, as are the accessories, except for the locomotive alongside the engine shed which dates from 1907. All are clockwork gauge 1 models.

RIGHT:
RIGHT:
Two typical early Bing locomotives in London North Western Railway livery for the British market and dating from the end of the nineteenth century.

BELOW:
Cast iron construction became popular in America, and here are two early models by Ives in that material.

for children in the first instance, adult interest was there from the start. Indeed, only reasonably affluent people could afford the most superior models offered by Bassett-Lowke and others since their price well exceeded the average monthly wage. In 1909 Bassett-Lowke started the first magazine aimed at model railway enthusiasts, *Models, Railways, and Locomotives*, edited by Lowke himself and Henry Greenly. Bassett-Lowke also opened up the first model shop in London, most of which was dedicated to model railways. For many years (until the 1870s) it was located at 112 High Holborn, complete with a distinctive signal gantry trade sign outside. It was generally considered to be the best-known model railway shop in the world (though Polks in New York ran it a close second) and much was made of the many famous people who were model railway enthusiasts and were among its customers. They included the future kings Edward VIII and George VI, members of the Siamese royal family, and Indian maharajahs. In 1906 Bassett-Lowke published *The Model Railway Handbook*, a compendium of information and ideas for the dedicated model railway enthusiast, and editions of this appeared into the 1950s. In 1910, as a result of a suggestion in *Models, Railways, and Locomotives*, a group of modelers in London formed the first recorded model railway club, with Henry Greenly as chairman. As it was the only one at the time, it was called 'The Model Railway Club', a title it has proudly retained even though there are now thousands of other model railway clubs around the world.

Model railways were now well accepted by the public. One enormous boost for the hobby must have been a huge promotion negotiated in 1908 and 1909 between Bassett-Lowke and the Caledonian Railway. In this deal Carette of Nuremburg made 30,000 tinplate O gauge clockwork models of the Caledonian's handsome new *Cardean* 4-6-0 express locomotive and a CR coach which went on sale at low 'pocket money' prices at all Caledonian Railway bookstalls, stations, and other outlets. Surviving examples of these are prized collectors' pieces today. Another promotional item was produced by Bing, also through Bassett-Lowke, and comprised a complete London North Western Railway train of a *King George V* 4-4-0 and five coaches all in a presentation box. By chance, this unpowered model was about the same scale as todays N gauge models (1:150), and are prized and charming collectors' pieces today.

The LNWR promotional model was a rare early example of models smaller than O gauge. Miniaturisation clearly had not been ignored, however, for it is recorded that Schoenner introduced some very small scale models in 1902, but they found no acceptance in the trade and no big production took place.

This first classic era of model railways came to an end, more or less, when the Great War started in August 1914. Supplies from the main producers in Germany disappeared in Britain and firms like Bassett-Lowke were forced to turn over to war work. Trade generally eased down for the duration of the war, though activity did not cease.

Collecting early models

Quite clearly it is no easy matter for anyone new to model railways to build up a collection of early models. They come on to the market via private sellers or through auction houses, and prices are extremely high. Very many surviving models are in museum or private collections and rarely leave them. By today's standards production runs were quite low (and may have been only in single figures in some cases). Big-run models, like the miniature Bing LNWR train, do turn up because they were made in much greater numbers. Occasionally old model trains dating from before about 1920 are found in antique shops, and no doubt there are still attics containing early model trains that have yet to see the light of day. The same applies to the printed ephemera of those days, though old catalogs and copies of early publications, such as

ABOVE:
Typical of the charm and ingenuity of many toy train items of the early days is this working ticket machine which was in the Märklin range c.1895.

Models, Railways, and Locomotives (which for a period was called *Model Railways and Locomotives*) can be found in secondhand book shops. This magazine closed down in 1919. But many early catalogs have been reprinted in facsimile form, particularly those of the German firms like Märklin and Bing, and these can be found in specialist railway bookshops.

If battered old models are found, they often need careful restoration, and there are firms and dealers who specialize in this. An interesting notion, however, very much aimed at those who like the charm of the old models, is a modern equivalent made in the old style. The foremost exponent of this art is Horst Reichert of Würtemberg, a true craftsman in tinplate, who makes exquisite gauge O and gauge 1 models, mainly German and French, in the style of Bing, Carette, and the other early firms. These are not replicas, and modern standards are used for the wheels, fittings, and mechanisms, but being made of tinplate they are strongly reminiscent of 1900-1914 models and have similar charm and character. They are more acceptably to scale, however, for today's enthusiast. All items are made in short runs to order. A few other specialists have also offered replicas of early Märklin and other models in recent years.

CHAPTER THREE
Models for the Masses

Many changes took place in the years following World War 1. Several of the German model train makers, including Carette and Schoenner had fallen victim to the wartime economy. German products were no longer welcomed overseas, and economic conditions as a result of the war had an effect on spending power and spending patterns.

This gaping hole in the model railway market was filled by the British Meccano Company. Frank Hornby had introduced a clever engineering toy, 'Mechanics Made Easy', soon renamed Meccano, in 1908. This became very popular and acquired a good reputation. Just as World War 1 started the company moved into a large purpose-built factory at Binns Road, Liverpool, England. Though Meccano production did not entirely cease during the war, most of the company output was con-

cerned with war work. Hornby had already planned to expand the range with motors and accessory items and one notion was model trains that could be assembled with nuts and bolts in the spirit of the Meccano constructional system. The first models, known as Hornby Trains, were announced in the summer of 1920 for the Christmas season sales. The first sets comprised a simple but robust 0-4-0 loco, a tender, and a coal wagon, plus an oval of plug-together tinplate track. These simple models could be unbolted and taken apart, but no real assembly variation was possible. The first locos came in black, red, and green, options depicting the popular LNWR, MR, and GNR companies. Further colors came later (blue for CR, brown for LBSCR), plus some export models marked for French companies. Parallel with the 'constructional'

RIGHT:
Hornby cardboard advertising stands for point-of-sale use in shops marked the application of advanced marketing techniques in 1937. These are replicas, but collecting this sort of promotional material is a specialized aspect of the hobby. In front of the adverts is the widely-sold O gauge M3 0-4-0 tank engine which, in different finishes, remained in the range until Hornby O gauge production ceased in the 1960s.

train set, Hornby produced a cheap tin printed clockwork train which was a very close copy of the cheapest Bing products, as was the track.

The new Hornby trains, all genuinely made in Britain, caught the patriotic peacetime mood and sold well, for the next 20 years or so. In 1921 the original 0-4-0 loco was improved, given a bigger clockwork motor and designated the No 1 loco. A more ambitious No 2 loco was produced for the 1921 Christmas season, a 4-4-0, again closely copied from Bing's design. Also released were Pullman cars and covered vans. Again, a range of colors corresponding to the most famous British companies was provided for the locomotive though it only carried a Meccano trademark. The freight stock was marked in various company styles, however, such as MR, LNWR, and GN, and a footbridge produced that year was the very first accessory.

For 1922 the cheap tin printed train set gave way to what was called the 'Zulu' series with a tender engine and a tank engine, initially both without reverse mechanism. These were stove enameled rather than tin printed (and it should be observed that

Hornby did more stove enameling as opposed to tin printing than most tinplate train makers). The Zulu tank engine was particularly good looking and is a prized collector's piece today, especially in its later reversing form. In 1923 the range grew to include a 4-4-4 tank engine, several more freight vehicles, coaches, signals, and a station. Hornby's collection expanded yearly throughout the 1920s with a change after 1923 to the 'Big Four' company colors and markings for both locomotives and rolling stock GWR, SR, LNER, and LMS. Accessories abounded: tunnels, fences, level crossings and just about everything else needed for an ambitious layout. Export activity was good, too, with a range of French wagons and locomotives in French markings. In 1927 the Meccano factory in the United States started to produce American-style models for that huge market. This project was short-lived, and in 1930 production moved back to England. The American Hornby models are, naturally, quite rare. In 1930 Hornby also began making Canadian-marked models, and through the 1930s suitably marked and liveried models were exported to Denmark, New Zealand,

ABOVE:
The Hornby No 1 locomotive of 1921 in one of its color options but with a Meccano trademark, hauling a contemporary Hornby open wagon in LNWR finish.

ABOVE:

*A postwar French
Hornby gauge O electric
locomotive with French
Hornby Wagons-Lits
Pullman coach. These
models were made in
the Hornby factory at
Bobigny, France.*

South Africa, Holland, Switzerland, and Sweden. The very first export customer had been Argentina in 1922; if this sounds unlikely it should be recalled that British companies had engineered and supplied most of the Argentine rail network.

All the early Hornby O gauge output was clockwork, but in 1925 the first electric train set appeared, appropriately with a Metropolitan Railway electric locomotive as the motive power. The track and general style of electrification was influenced by Lionel's electric train sets in America, but the set worked on a hazardous high voltage only ineffectively reduced from the mains, so subsequent sets, including the Metropolitan one, were given a 4 volt motor operated from a battery accumulator. Electric versions of most of the other locomotives appeared and 6 volt motors were later fitted. In 1931 a new electrical system of 20 volts with a proper mains transformer and controler, similar to the modern style, was introduced.

Significant years were 1929 and 1930 when superior modern-looking No 1 Special tender and tank locomotives were added to the range, as well as four close-to-scale models of 'Big Four' locomotives. These were the Midland Compound (LMS), L1 (SR), *County of Bedford* (GWR), and *Yorkshire* (LNER), all 4-4-0s and very desirable collectors' pieces today. They were designated No 2 Special. The 4-4-4 tank engine was replaced with a modern-looking 4-4-2T (No 2 Special Tank). Much less satisfactory from an aesthetic point of view were the No 3 engines, 4-4-2 express types based on a French design and introduced for a French 'Blue Train' set, but also finished in 'Big Four' British colors, one for each regional company. These models, *Royal Scot, Flying Scotsman, Lord Nelson,* and *Caerphilly Castle* still baffle newcomers today since they bear no resemblance to the famous locomotives whose names they carry.

During the 1930s the small Zulu-type locomotives were replaced with more topical 'No 1' tank and tender engines of the 0-4-0 type that remained in the range, under various designations, until Hornby tinplate production ceased in the late 1960s. Manufactured in their thousands, they are probably the most common surviving Hornby types. Probably the most famous British manufacturer, Hornby's range ran into hundreds of models and variations, both clockwork and electric and its impact on the toy market was considerable.

The Hornby O gauge No 1 Special Locomotive in LMS finish in its 20 volt AC electric form. This is a beautifully restored example.

BELOW:
The true flavor of 1930s model railways is given by this Hornby layout scene featuring Hornby Southern Railway locomotives, including the L1 4-4-0, signals, and engine sheds and accessories. This is a 20 volt AC electric layout.

RIGHT:
Two of the prewar editions of the famous Hornby Book of Trains, *together with a similar style postwar book devoted to Hornby-Dublo.*

Marketing was brilliant, with attractive catalogs and point-of-sale material, a splendid *Hornby Book of Trains* published annually until World War 2, the *Meccano Magazine* carrying monthly articles, and a Hornby Railway Company that all Hornby owners could join. There were even Hornby sweaters and badges, and other items, a marketing scheme that was advanced for its day but commonplace today. Dinky Toys, first produced in the mid-1930s, developed into a vast model vehicle range in their own right, but the original concept was as accessories supporting the Hornby train range and included numerous figures and other items for use on rail layouts.

Hornby O gauge models had such wide charm and appeal, and played such a big part in so many childhoods, that they are remembered with particular affection today. The models still turn up from family hoards, but there is a vigorous secondhand market for them and, provided you can afford today's high prices, building up a Hornby train collection is still a very practical proposition. As a much-reduced Hornby range remained in production into the 1960s (the very last were made in 1969), there are more Hornby O

gauge items still around to be traded than most other long discontinued model train ranges of the past.

The coming of small scales

With Hornby dominating the popular market for tinplate trains in Britain and the Commonwealth after World War 1, Bassett-Lowke, having lost their German manufacturing partners, at first had to use their own resources to produce their gauge O and gauge 1 models. They began to manufacture more track, locomotives and rolling stock than they had done before the war and acquired some press tools from the defunct Carette company to help. However, the company had worked so closely with Bing that an order placed in 1914 was delivered in 1919 (at 1914 prices) and large follow-up orders were placed with the Germany company. These failed to sell so well, largely because of the changing spending habits and living conditions in postwar Britain. Money was tighter, and so was space. New houses were smaller, so space for model layouts was more difficult to find.

W. J. Bassett-Lowke sensed that smaller models were needed. While a few very small models had been produced in earlier years, there had been no great effort to popularize the idea. Bassett-Lowke got together with Bing once more, and with Henry Greenly involved in the design, a new toy train system, and scale, was evolved. What they did, in effect, was to take the then smallest scale, O gauge, and halve it. So the 7mm to 1ft scale of O gauge became 3.5mm to 1ft in the new small scale. The 1¼in. track gauge therefore became ⅝in., later changed to a metric 16.5mm. The new scale was called variously, even by Bassett-Lowke, HO (for 'Half O') or OO gauge. The new system, called the Bing Table Railway, was small enough to be just that. You could set up a reasonable layout on a table top, because everything was an eighth the size, by volume, of O gauge. A small locomotive would stand on the palm of the hand, which was not possible with O gauge or larger models.

The new system was put on the market in 1922 with a range of 11 boxed sets and many accessories, all modestly priced. Bing's usual manufacturing techniques were used; models were in printed tinplate, and the propulsion was initially clockwork, though later a 6 volt electric version was produced. All the models were very toy-like, rather like miniatures of the cheaper O gauge tinplate trains. The locomotive bore a superficial resemblance to a London North Western Railway 2-4-0 tank engine and as usual, the loco was available in the colors of the leading British companies, with freight stock similarly marked. There was also a series in Deutsche Reichsbahn colors for Germany, and some runs were made in French and American markings for those export markets.

The design was quite ingenious. The lineside structures and accessories all clipped to the track, and the track was made in tinplate by folding up from a single sheet of metal. The only problem was the crude toy-like nature of the models. They have an immensely innocent charm for today's collector, but they were no more than caricatures of the real thing. This must have limited sales, as the range had disappeared from the market by the late 1920s. However, the Bing Table Railway was very significant in the history of model railways and the models have an appeal to today's collector for that reason. The system popularized the notion that a good model railway in a small scale had lots of potential, it solved the space and cost problem, and it

made model railways accessible to many more enthusiasts as a result. More than that, it captured the imagination of some very keen modelers who saw that they could build on the Bing Table Railway idea to produce something of much superior scale appearance. In 1925 the first magazine exclusively devoted to the smaller gauges of model railways was produced. *Model Railway News*, edited and published by Percival Marshall, carried this message to the keenest model railway enthusiasts in Britain and overseas.

Through the pages of the early issues of this magazine, several enthusiasts showed how the new small HO scale and gauge could be used to make true scale models. A. R. Walkley was a master of the HO concept. He built what was probably the first true scale HO layout, a folding layout called 'The Railway in a Suitcase', using principles that are still used today more than 70 years later. Walkley also built a true scale HO locomotive and developed the principle of automatic coupling and uncoupling that, in an evolved form, is still used on British OO gauge models today. Stewart Reidpath, another enthusiast for the new small scale, went into business supplying compo-

ABOVE:
A complete operating layout built by collector Bert Pollard in the 1980s from Bing Table Railway equipment of the early 1920s to give modern enthusiasts a good idea of what early small scale railway modeling was like.

nents and kits for HO, which was established formally as 1:87 scale, 16.5mm gauge.

The new small scale still took some years to get firmly established, for only the most dedicated enthusiast with sufficient modeling skill could really take advantage of the limited components on offer. Scale track, for example, had to be hand made – the Bing track was far too crude. A further complication occurred with a controversy that still endures today, known generally as 'The Battle of the Gauges'. This rolled on right through the 1930s and beyond. In essence it was found that British models made to exact 1:87 scale were too small in body and narrow in width to fit over the commercially made motors, wheels, and chassis then available, even to most scratch-builders. Henry Greenly, who had a big influence due to his Bassett-Lowke connections, was a practical engineer rather than a scale purist, and he suggested that the simple answer to the problem was to increase the scale of British HO size models from 3.5mm to 1ft up to 4mm to 1 foot. This small increment made the models sufficiently large in body to fit over the wheels and chassis. Unfortunately, however, the gauge remained the same and in scale terms 16.5mm became just

over 4ft instead of 4ft 8½ in. The 'new' scale was called OO to distinguish from HO.

Arguments ranged for years from purists who thought the scale and gauge should stay at the true HO relationship of 1:87/16.5mm and those happy to accept the compromise OO gauge of 1:76 scale/16.5mm gauge. Only the track was common to the two. The trade suppliers chose to follow the pragmatic Greenly solution, so British HO almost died out, only kept going to this day by a few keen enthusiasts.

Elsewhere in the world events took a different course. In the United States the idea of HO took an early hold, though enthusiasts at first could only get supplies from Britain. In the 1920s the American market was dominated by Lionel, with O gauge and their 'Standard' gauge of 2⅛in. (53mm), and rivals like American Flyer, who were still very much tinplate-orientated in standard (though many of their models were die-cast or in cast iron). The British HO scale approach was appreciated by keen American modelers, one of the keenest being Allan Lake Rice who did much to promulgate early ideas. The British OO gauge idea also got to the United States, but there they saw the wisdom of increasing the

RIGHT:
A closer view of some Bing Table Railway equipment, the first commercial HO-size trains. The LMS 2-4-0 is clockwork, but electric versions were also produced. The buildings were part of the fully integrated range. Everything is in printed tinplate.

track gauge to scale as well, so ended up with a track gauge for OO of 19mm. In America, in fact, there were no real dimensional problems in either scale because American trains are so much bigger and wider than British trains that whether reduced to 1:87 scale (HO) or 1:76 scale (OO), the wheels and motors fit comfortably within the dimensions.

The fact that model railways were now becoming a serious hobby and not just an extension of nursery playtime was emphasized by the growth of model railway clubs and societies from the mid-1920s onward. In Britain another journal appeared in 1930, *Model Railway Constructor*, and in America the first magazine exclusively devoted to model railways appeared in 1934, the still-celebrated *Model Railroader*, published and edited by a pioneer enthusiast, Al Kalmbach. Several companies who became well-known names were established between the wars to cater for the serious enthusiast with kits and components, mostly for the small scales (0/ HO/OO), among them Hamblings, Bonds, Gem, Cimco, W & H (Great Britain), and Walthers, Varney, Lobaugh, and Mantua (USA). In the later part of the 1930s, some British enthusiasts were worrying about the scale-to-gauge discrepancy of OO, and a few models were made with a track gauge of 18mm instead of 16.5mm, with track to match, of course. Though these models were advertised and discussed, the number of modelers actually moving to the more accurate gauge must have been very small, for few prewar models so modified have come to light.

Commercial development of HO in Europe was largely led by Germany in the 1930s. In 1935 the mighty Märklin company, seeing the way interest was increasing in the smaller scale, introduced a complete system which they initially called OO gauge, though in those days scale was not too precise as the early models were a little toy-like. Although the Märklin models were tinplate they looked a lot better than Bing's earlier efforts and more like the real thing. They used 20 volt AC electric with a center third rail (later changed to stud contact which made the center pick-up look less obvious). All the models were based, in outline if not in chassis (for most were four-wheelers) on Deutsche Reichsbahn types, but for export to Britain the same models were made in 'Big Four' company colors. For the American market they were in an American-style finish with a

RIGHT:
Early issues of the British *Model Railway News,* and bottom, an early issue of the American *Model Railroader,* this being the first edition to carry a color cover.

ABOVE:
Five Bassett-Lowke publications, including an early Model Railway Handbook.

BELOW:
A 1920 gauge O Kraus Fandor loco hauling two Dorfan coaches.

few American fittings – customers in those days were more tolerant of 'near enough' finishes and detail than they would be today. Later, some more precise models were made for export markets. One of the rarest of all Märklin models is a smart Midland Compound locomotive for OO gauge which was made in small numbers in 1938.

A much bigger impact was made at the time by a rival system, the Trix Twin Railway. Stefan Bing was Jewish, and under Hitler's

regime, the Bing company was forced to close and Bing himself went into exile, coming to England to make use of his commercial contacts with Bassett-Lowke. Some remaining Bing directors (who were Aryan) stayed in Germany and set up a new company, Trix, to carry on the Bing mantle. Trix not only produced a construction set of the Meccano type, but under the influence of W. J. Bassett-Lowke also designed and tooled up the Trix Twin Railway system in HO, again billed as a 'table railway'. The unique feature of Trix Twin was that the center third rail was the common electrical return and the two outer rails each carried a separate circuit. Two locomotives could be individually controled on the same track if their respective pick-up shoes were set to brush one or other of the outer rails. No other wiring was necessary. Later a third locomotive could be controled if it was picked up by pantograph from overhead wiring. At the time this 'twin' control concept, which was quite ingenious, excited much attention and gave Trix a commercial edge. All the early models were German style, of course, for their home market, but Stefan Bing in England set up British Trix which produced British-style bodies for the locomotives and British-style rolling stock. The original

Trix models were introduced in 1935 in German-style only, and were followed by the British Trix models in 1937, and American locomotives and stock for the U.S. market.

While the Trix models were well accepted, like the old Bing table models they were quite crude in scale terms and the bright tinplate track on a Bakelite base was extremely unrealistic. The overall concept of the range which included delightful Art Deco structures was much appreciated, however, and today there are a lot of Trix collectors and a thriving Trix Twin society.

The Meccano company had obviously watched these German developments with interest and saw that the failing of both Märklin and Trix models was in their quite crude appearance which was just not realistic enough to attract the true scale enthusiast. Meccano launched their OO gauge model railway system for Christmas 1938 with some very attractive models indeed, such as a splendid Gresley A4 streamlined Pacific and a tank engine that quite closely resembled a Gresley 0-6-2T N2 class engine, but was just nondescript enough to look acceptable when finished in any Big Four company colors. The range was called Hornby-Dublo, a neat play on the track gauge name, and all the models were of good scale appearance – sensationally good by comparison with the rivals. Serious enthusiasts could go for these and did, and the range enjoyed the same success as the previous Meccano products like Hornby O gauge trains and Dinky Toys. Initially the models

ABOVE:
Märklin King George V built for Bassett-Lowke and the British market in 1935 and displaying the famous bell that this locomotive carried as a memento of its American tour.

LEFT:
A gauge O Lionel 2-4-2 electric loco with two Pullman cars and an observation car from 1936. Lionel still remains one of the most famous of American model railway names.

43

were offered with clockwork or electric traction. The rolling stock was printed tinplate, but remarkably well done for the time. It still looks much more acceptable today than the other contemporary small scale offerings. Meccano's only mistake, though they did not then recognize it, was the adoption of center third rail pick-up, this and the track style being based on Märklin's style.

The larger scales

The coming of the small scales did not eclipse the larger scales. In the United States Lionel, Ives, and American Flyer were the three biggest producers, all with O gauge ranges and the larger 'standard' gauge (2⅛in.) which was unique to America. These were all to 'toy' standards, like Hornby in Britain. Today Lionel still survives after various changes of ownership and still produces O gauge models to these 'toy' standards. Though of limited interest to scale enthusiasts, there is a vast following for Lionel from collectors, and after so many decades of production there is a great deal to collect. A new gauge was introduced in America in 1937, known as S gauge which was

intermediate in size between HO and O gauge. The scale was ³⁄₁₆in. to one foot which made it half the scale of gauge 1, and for a time in Great Britain this gauge was known as 'H1' ('half one gauge'). The track gauge was therefore ⅞in. (22mm) and the scale reduction was 1:64. Being of American origin, non-metric measurements have commonly been used for S gauge. The scale was put on a commercial footing by the Cleveland Model Company who wished to diversify from the aircraft kits which were their main product. The Cleveland model trains were therefore made from wood, like model airplanes, and came in kit form. Initially the locomotives were not powered, and Cleveland called it CD gauge in order to publicize their name. The size of S gauge quickly caught the imagination of American enthusiasts and other companies got involved. American Flyer, later merged with another firm called Gilbert, produced a 'toy train' range in S gauge which really popularized the scale. The AF models, though to 'toy' standards, were of much better scale appearance than most others of this type. The American Flyer range in S gauge has managed

BELOW:
A tinplate Atlantic 2-4-2 from the Lionel Standard Gauge range.

to survive to modern times under various owners. Numerous other firms in America supplied kits and components over the years and S gauge still has a firm following in America with its own magazines and suppliers and a firm (American Models) which today produces excellent scale ready-to-run plastic models and ready-to-lay track.

S gauge remains largely American in commercial terms, but a British pioneer, Charles Wynne, developed and built the first true scale S gauge models to ³⁄₁₆in. scale (called H1 in Britain) in the early 1920s. His first working model was a fine 1:64 scale replica of the famous Midland Railway 4-4-0 locomotive No 999 which he described and illustrated in the October 1923 issue of the magazine *Everyday Science*. There is a small but keen S Gauge Model Railway Society in Britain which has long championed S gauge, but the British modeler in this delightful scale has to work largely from scratch supported by a few components, such as wheels and fittings, available from the society.

Bassett-Lowke continued to supply the gauge O and gauge 1 enthusiast, despite the excursions into smaller scales. Some beautiful live steam models were produced, the most famous being a very superior Mogul 2-6-0 of scale appearance. It was produced in LNER, MR, GWR, and SR forms with fittings and finish appropriate to each company, though the changes were achieved by the crafty use of varied details with common main components. Electric and clockwork versions appeared, as well as live steam, and in various forms this model remained in production until the Bassett-Lowke firm in its original form ceased production in the 1960s. Gauge 1 versions of this model were also available. Equally well-known were the 'Enterprise' 4-4-0 and 'Super Enterprise' 4-6-0 live steamers. These were freelance models with simple oscillating steam mechanisms, and were much more toy-like that the Mogul. The 4-6-0, however, had a close resemblance to the LMS *Royal Scot* and SR *Lord Nelson* and was finished as these types. These models could also be purchased as kits for home construction.

Bassett-Lowke also built very large scale models for display and passenger-carrying

BELOW:
Three models from the American Flyer O gauge range of the 1930s. The cast iron clockwork tank locomotive, front left, lettered GNR was produced for the British market under the name 'British Flyer'. It had an inappropriate tender which this model has lost.

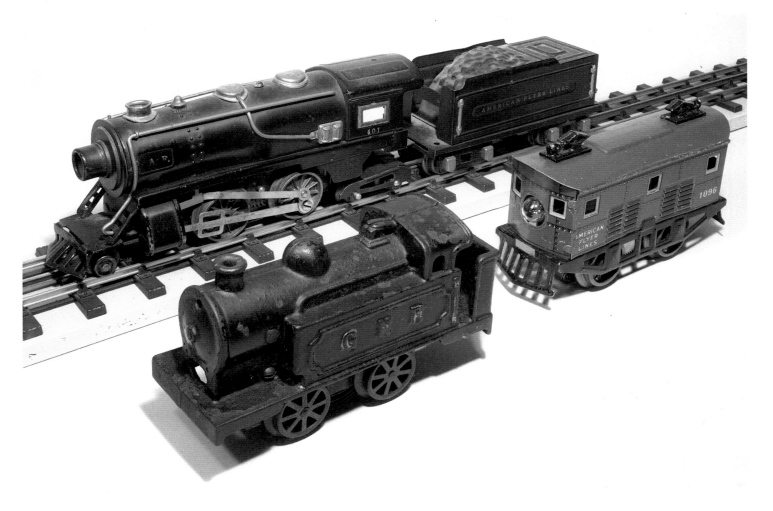

RIGHT:
A favorite model for many years was the Bassett-Lowke O gauge Mogul, this being the LMS version in its clockwork form.

BELOW:
Gauge O models with litho-printed paper sides for coaches and wagons from the 1930s.

purposes, some being produced for private estates. Some of these survive (and some remain in use), but at the more commercial level there was a continual release of various O gauge models. When Bing ceased operations in Germany in the 1930s, Märklin made some interesting British-type models for the Bassett-Lowke range. There were big orders, too, in both 1926 and 1932 for large runs of clockwork 4-4-0 locomotives for low price promotions (collect coupons and get a model locomotive) for the BDV and Kensitas cigarette firms. The rather pleasing 4-4-0 tinplate model produced for these schemes remained in the Bassett-Lowke range into the 1960s, latterly in British Railways finish as *Prince Charles*. This modest model would be worth looking for now as representative of Bassett-Lowke's great days in O gauge.

Two other well-known British names were Bowman and Leeds. Bowman made some rather overscale live steam models of engineering interest, but of no great charm to the enthusiast for realistic models.

The Leeds Model Company, founded in 1921, with the energetic R. F. Stedman as its guiding light, flourished between the two world wars (and continued for some years after World War 2) and produced O gauge models of British types of great charm and realism, even though some of the locomotives were a little truncated. The rolling stock was particularly good. Leeds were early users of plastics in model making, but they also used wood construction with realistic printed color litho overlays to get good scale effects. Leeds models are much sought-after today and a trust looks after the old Leeds interests and ensures the famous name survives.

In the last few years of the 1930s the model railway hobby was developing fast. They were exciting times. In the United States the firms of Varney and Mantua had become well established as makers of HO kits and models of high standard, much in advance of what could be bought elsewhere. The Lionel firm moved into American OO gauge (19mm) with a fine 'Hudson' loco and range of rolling stock which is highly valued today. Scalecraft was another leading name in American OO gauge, and numerous firms produced O gauge models and kits at that time. All this was helped by the formation in 1935 of a nationwide organization for modelers, the NMRA

BELOW:
Gauge O Bowman 0-4-0 steam tank locos, a 300 twin cylinder version, a 410 single cylinder, and a LNER goods brake van of 1935. The locomotives still run as well as ever despite being over 60 years old.

TOP:
Lionel OO gauge New York Central Hudson 4-6-4.

ABOVE:
Hornby O gauge Eton *'Schools' class 4-4-0 20 volt AC electric loco of 1937.*

(National Model Railroaders Association) who liaised with manufacturers and helped formulate scale standards and procedures, all to the great advantage of American hobbyists.

In Germany Märklin had developed their HO range to a high standard and were now producing models of good scale appearance, a match for Hornby-Dublo in looks. The firm was also making a glittering selection of gauge O and gauge 1 models, much better than anything they had made before. And Hornby gauge O was still advancing with two classic locomotives released in the late 1930s, the SR 'Schools' 4-4-0 *Eton* and the superb, and now much-prized Stanier Pacific *Princess Elizabeth*. British OO gauge was being mightily encouraged by small suppliers, and one of the leading British modelers of the time was

Edward Beal, whose West Midlands layout and many articles inspired many enthusiasts.

Collecting interwar models

Model railway equipment made between the two world wars is generally easier to find – at a price – than pre-1914 equipment. Hornby tinplate gauge O is, in relative terms, plentiful in Britain and the countries to which it was exported and is probably the most common of models of this period. Märklin and Bing models turn up less frequently, and Lionel is probably the most frequently seen of the American output of those days. Even so, all this material has to be sought out either through specialist dealers or at model shows or sale rooms. Much easier to acquire are magazines and catalogs of the era, often

found in secondhand shops specializing in transport subjects.

Nothing is impossible, however, as British collector Bert Pollard discovered in the late 1980s when he became interested in the Bing Table Railway of 1922 vintage. In just four years, starting with nothing, but by assiduous searching and advertising, he managed to acquire virtually every model and variation in the range, despite the fact that the average modeler today would consider these little Bing models impossible to find. As a result of his searches Pollard was able to build a complete Bing layout in the style of the 1920s which is often seen and admired at model railway shows.

If you cannot match this level of luck and effort, there are some opportunities which will give you a link, at least, with the past. Pre-war Hornby-Dublo models are hard to find as production was cut short by the war and changes were made afterwards. But the Wrenn 0-6-2T sold today is made with the same tooling as the 1938 original, so if you get that you have a direct relic from the past, with only the coupling and minor parts different. If you collect Hornby-Dublo, though, beware of fakes which are recent Wrenn products with added Hornby-Dublo markings and a consequent increase in the selling price. In 1985, Märklin made a delightful series of replicas of their original 1935 HO models using the original tooling, and it is easier to find these than the 1935 originals, of course. At least one specialist firm in Germany makes replicas of old Märklin O gauge.

ABOVE:
A popular 'private owner' van subject is the Colman's Mustard van, and is shown here in gauge N, OO, O, and 2 versions. The N and OO models are both made by Peco, the gauge O model is Hornby tinplate; the second (rear) O gauge model and the gauge 2 model are scratch-built models based on the Peco van. Colorful private owner markings have always been attractive to collectors.

CHAPTER FOUR
Model Railways Come of Age

The outbreak of World War 2 put a brake on model railway development from about 1940 to 1948, for even after the war ended in 1945 there were several years of austerity before any sort of consumer production resumed on a meaningful scale. The war did not stop the hobby, however, for model production did not finally cease until 1941 when all the European and American makers were engaged in war work. Modelers kept going, for constructive hobbies were a theraputic aid to the boredom and hazards of war duty. Small components for scratch-building could still be obtained and there was much ingenuity in working with cardboard and scrap items. The period is not without interest to the collector as there were several model items produced, largely card-based because there was a ban on using metal for model-making.

Card cut-out manufacturers in Britain included Micromodels, a neat little series that covered many subjects including railways. The card trains which could be made from these cut-outs give miniatures about the size of the later Märklin Z gauge models. Model-craft made card cut-out vehicles, and ERG made a big range of card cut-out rolling stock kits for both OO and O gauges. There were litho overlays for rolling stock (they had been started by Modelcraft in the 1930s) which could fit on card or scrap wood bodies, and in the late 1940s embossed card OO and HO rolling stock kits appeared in both Britain and the USA, as well as the realistic range of Bilteezi card cut-out structures, introduced by Hamblings.

Firms like Peco (track components), ERG, and S & B became well-known in Britain for keeping the hobby going with all the bits and pieces for scratch-builders in these difficult years. It was not until the Christmas season of 1948 that the British market saw Hornby, Hornby-Dublo, and Trix Twin back in production, though the ranges were reduced from their prewar sizes. In 1949-50 a new firm called Graham Farish appeared on the scene and made quite an impact. By the standards of the day their models looked very realistic. Such types as a Stanier 'Black Five' 4-6-0, GWR Prairie 2-6-2 tank loco, and a Bulleid Pacific appeared in die-cast metal in OO gauge, along with a good choice of rolling stock. The new and significant idea from this company was Formoway flexible ready-to-lay track, sold by the yard and pinned down on the baseboard. It was a more attractive alternative to the restrictions of sectional track

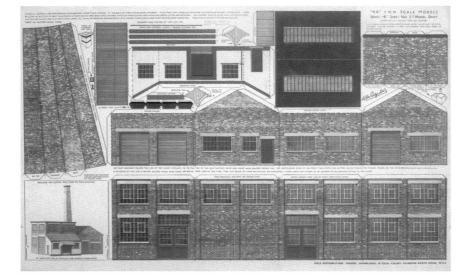

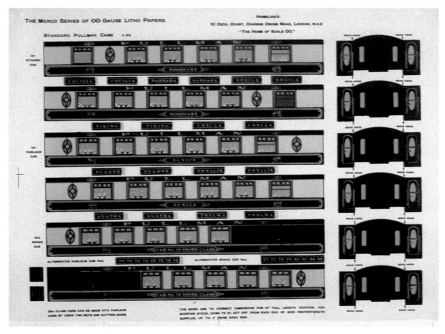

with its fixed geometry, for flexible track allowed transitional curves and gentle radii just like the real thing, and by all previous standards it looked very realistic. In those days the sleepers (cross-ties) were in fiber which warped in a damp atmosphere. Before flexible track it was necessary to buy components and make scale track laboriously by hand. The flexible track put realistic layouts in reach of all and could reasonably be called a milestone in the history of model railways. Other firms produced flexible track, among them, Peco, who soon came to dominate the British market and replaced the fiber cross-ties with the much more durable and more realistic plastic cross-ties. Farish later moved into N gauge in the 1960s and became the leading British maker in this scale.

An even bigger impact on the hobby in Britain was made by a small firm called Rovex which appeared in 1950 with an all-plastic OO gauge train in a two-rail 12 volt DC system. The first models were a 'Princess' Pacific and LMS coaches. Limited production was sold

LEFT:
More attractive card cut-outs of the 1940s were the Micromodels which became very well known. These made unpowered trains about the size of today's Z gauge models.

BELOW:
Graham Farish made a big impact in the early 1950s with their OO gauge range and flexible track. Shown here are the 'Black Five' and the 'King', two of the best-known models.

ABOVE:
This OO gauge New York Central Hudson was made by the British firm Graham Farish for the export market.

RIGHT:
A very early example of the Hornby-Dublo Duchess of Atholl without smoke deflectors, scheduled for production in 1939-40 but not actually made until 1948 when post-war production resumed. The Hornby-Dublo range survived into the early 1960s.

out for Christmas 1950, but the plastic chassis caused problems and was replaced with metal for 1951. Motors came from a firm called Zenith. In May 1951 Rovex trains made a big hit at the British Industries fair and orders outstripped the capacity of the small Rovex company. Late in 1951 it joined the large Lines Brothers (Triang) toy group and from May 1952, with big marketing support, a much enlarged range was launched as Triang Railways, though the Rovex name was also still used. The Zenith company also joined the group and their neat motor design was much used elsewhere as well as for the Triang models.

Business with Triang Railways was so good that in 1954 the company moved into a huge purpose-built factory at Margate, Kent. Through the 1950s and 1960s Triang Railways flourished, and the range grew to a considerable size, all in OO gauge. There was a further range for export, scaled in HO and called the 'Transcontinental' series, based on various trains from overseas. Though some of these were nondescript, there were also some fine models of actual types such as the then new American Budd diesel railcar. At this peak

period, Triang also had factories or license-production operations in Australia, France, South Africa, and New Zealand.

Triang Railways, cheaper and with two-rail tracks, provided serious competition to Hornby-Dublo who, nevertheless, did quite well in the 1950s and also expanded considerably. The 1950-52 period saw production restrictions enforced by the demand for metal in armaments for the Korean War. The die-cast and tinplate construction methods of prewar days put Hornby-Dublo at a disadvantage in terms of production costs against Triang's cheaper plastic designs. The Dublo range was never as big as Triang's either. In 1959-60 Hornby-Dublo switched over to two-rail to compete better with Triang, as two-rail electrification was much more realistic than center third-rail. The Meccano group was by now in financial decline, however, and Triang took them over in early 1964. The Triang-Hornby name emerged from this, but very little of the Dublo designs fitted in with Triang production methods. The old Hornby-Dublo range went to Wrenn, which was another company in the Lines Brothers group under different ownership, and, in the 1990s, still

BELOW:
Triang, later Triang-Hornby, Railways dominated the British OO gauge markets in the 1950s and 1960s. Here are some of the models and packaging and two key publications that the company put out in the 1960s.

producing the old Dublo designs for appreciative collectors.

Triang-Hornby continued to expand as Britain's leading model railway maker. There was a rocky period in the mid- to late-1960s when electric car racing temporarily snatched a big chunk of the leisure market. In late 1971 the mighty Lines Brothers group collapsed and another group, Dunbee-Combex-Marx, bought up the Rovex subsidiary; the range became known as Hornby. Only the name, however, linked it to the old Hornby ranges. Hornby O gauge production ceased when Meccano collapsed in 1964 and the last stocks were sold out in 1969. In 1982 the Dunbee-Combex-Marx group failed, Hornby became a separate company again by management buyout, and has retained its independence ever since. From the enthusiasts' point of view Triang/Triang-Hornby/Hornby in the 1960 to early 1980s period was a dominant force in the British model railway hobby. They did a lot of promotional work and succeeded in attracting young enthusiasts. With some models,

like the Bulleid Pacifics, Hymek diesel, and some 4-4-0s which repeated (in OO) the Hornby 4-4-0s of the 1930s, they also appealed to serious modelers. Smoke units, magnetic traction, operating, and early command control (Zero-One) were among the innovations from the company. They also perfected what has become the most widely used auto-coupler in Britain, the tension-lock type. This was derived from the original Walkley idea of the 1920s. Another popular British coupler in postwar Hornby-Dublo and Trix Twin days, was the Simplex, a compact auto-coupler designed by S. C. Pritchard of Peco. The British Trix company was a relatively minor segment of the postwar British market and had faded away by the early 1970s, despite an update in appearance and design which was very effective.

For the small-scale modeler in Britain there were at least two postwar boom periods. The first was the late 1950s and early 1960s when Triang were at their most prolific, and accessory and kit makers supplied an ever-

BELOW:
The top model in the Triang OO gauge range in the late 1960s was the Flying Scotsman *seen here in both LNER and British Railways finishes.*

The Hornby-Dublo Royal Mail coach set was typical of working accessories in that it could duplicate the collection and delivery of mailbags on the move just like the real thing.

BELOW:
Wrenn took over the old Hornby-Dublo range in the 1960s and continued production from the Hornby molds, typified by the Pullman car and Bulleid rebuilt Pacific shown here. The original Bulleid Pacific and the 'Royal Scot' (the two lower models) were new models by Wrenn in the Hornby-Dublo style.

increasing band of modelers. K's, Ratio, Wills, Gem, and Peco, the latter four still very important were established at this time. Kitmaster produced a plastic kit range, which offered locomotives and coaches at popular prices. Airfix, too, who had started with plastic airplane kits, also made fine inexpensive railway kits at pocket-money prices, and later on Airfix took over the Kitmaster models as well. Most of these plastic kits are still available, now under the Dapol name.

During the second boom of 1975-80 Airfix, Palitoy and the Italian Lima company all started big OO gauge ranges with details and finish superior to Hornby's. This caused Hornby to raise its standards, and the quality of off-the-shelf OO gauge models became remarkable and the choice extensive. Lima briefly made models in British HO at this time before realizing that OO gauge was dominant in Britain, but these HO models were also useful to the small band of Britons still faithful to HO. All this was too good to be true, and in the more turbulent financial conditions of the early 1980s, Airfix and Palitoy disappeared completely from the model railway scene. Fortunately most of what they produced reappeared under new brand names such as

Dapol, Replica, and Bachmann. In the 1990s, these names, with Hornby, still lead the large British OO gauge market.

British O gauge almost disappeared in the early postwar period. Though Bassett-Lowke carried on into the early 1960s, as did Leeds, sales of O gauge equipment were very low, and only the simpler Hornby O gauge tinplate remained in production at the same time. However, in the 1970s and 1980s there was a resurgence of interest through the Gauge O Guild, formed by enthusiasts in the late 1960s to save the gauge from extinction. Today the numbers of O gauge followers are counted in thousands and there are many small specialist suppliers (but no really big manufacturer) supporting the scale. Much the same happened with gauge 1 in Britain.

There was a brief interlude with the British version of a new gauge in the 1957-63 period when Triang made a range in TT (3mm to 1ft, 1:100 scale). These were attractive models, briefly popular and quite well-served by some kit and accessory makers as well. However, TT was possibly too close in size to OO to offer a genuine alternative. Big interest petered out, but has been kept going ever since by a very keen 3mm Society who produce kits, track,

RIGHT:
Models from the last years of British Trix: 'Britannia' and 56XX 0-6-2T (top), BR Standard Class 5 (center), and EM1 electric loco (bottom).

ABOVE:
Airfix made a big impact on the British market in the 1960s with a good range of inexpensive plastic assembly kits, of which this is one example with the made-up model top right. The kits were still available under the Dapol name in the 1990s. These models were all for OO gauge.

LEFT:
This O gauge Great Western ventilated van is made by Peco and is typical of the high standard of plastic kits available today.

16mm industrial narrow gauge engine from the American Loco Company.

and parts for members. When N gauge reached Britain in 1965-66 there was a happier story. Graham Farish made an early switch and became the leading British N gauge supplier, ably supported by Peco, Gem, and other kit and accessory makers, plus a flourishing N Gauge Society. The appearance of 'fine scale' for 4mm scale with P4/S4 standard (18.83mm) and EM (18.2mm), give a much better scale-to-gauge ratio than 16.5mm. However, only specialist suppliers cater for this and it is still the province of the more skilled and dedicated modeler.

The American Scene

Mantua and Varney had really put HO on the American map in the late 1930s. Varney was advertising a sprung HO chassis kit in 1940 and in the early postwar days when production resumed, a plastic-bodied Varney 'Docksider' 0-4-0 tank engine became a massive bestseller. Varney were one of the first to use plastic in the postwar era. The Varney company did not long survive the death of its innovative founder, Gordon Varney, in the early 1960s, but many of the former Varney molds and components survive in modern kit

ranges, such as Con-Cor. Walthers became an ever more prominent name on the product, accessory, and distribution scene, and is still the major player in this area. Other big names postwar were English, All-Nation, Midlin, Bowser, Ulrich, and Roundhouse of which the latter remains prominent both in HO and N. Most notable of all, however, is Athearn. Irv Athearn started in O gauge with kits in 1945, but HO was clearly the growing market, and by 1956 he had switched over completely to HO.

Today the Athearn range in HO offers superb value for money with good performing locomotives and a large choice of easy-to-assemble rolling stock kits all made to high standards in the USA at modest prices. American OO gauge faltered after World War 2 and today it is a rarity with very few adherents. But from the late 1960s onwards HO production expanded even further with models made overseas all coming on to the US market. AHM, Atlas, Con-Cor, Modelpower, Lifelike, and Bachmann are some of the names (not all still active) whose models were made variously in Italy, Germany, Austria, Yugoslavia, Taiwan, China, and Hong Kong.

In recent years the most revered name from overseas is Kato of Japan, who not only have their own ranges of Japanese HO and N gauge models, but have made superb models of American locomotives and rolling stock in both HO and N. Not only have they made models for American companies, but they also set up their own American subsidiary to sell models in the United States under their own name. Among the other makers, Bachmann, originally American, now Hong Kong-owned, has become a major player on the American HO and N scene in the past decade. They not only make large HO and N ranges of good quality but have moved into the larger G gauge and narrow O gauge. Bachmann also operate in Europe with both a British OO gauge range and a German/Swiss/French/Austrian HO range taken over from the former Austrian Liliput company.

N gauge has flourished in America since the late 1960s, S gauge is well served, and so is O gauge, though these two minority gauges are mainly served by smaller companies. In the early 1970s, however, both Atlas and Rivarossi (of Italy) made excellent American ready-to-run O gauge ranges which are collectors'

pieces today. As in Britain there was a brief period in the 1950s and 1960s when TT (⅒ in. to one foot, 1:120 scale) thrived. TT was, in fact, conceived and developed in America, the leading name being HP Products. TT stood for 'table top', yet another use of that term. A development in the 1980s was the widespread introduction of G gauge, and a rather hybrid gauge 1(1:29 scale instead of 1:32) to the American market, with Bachmann, LGB, Lionel, REA, and Roundhouse as main suppliers of equipment.

Europe

In the early postwar years Märklin and Trix resumed HO production and have continued ever since. They were joined by Fleischmann, a long-established toy maker, who started with O gauge in 1950 and switched over to HO in 1952. In the late 1960s they also moved into N gauge with the Piccolo range, and in the 1990s they added a rather pleasing 16.5mm narrow gauge range to their output, mainly intended for children but also of interest to serious modelers. Despite the fact that 1:87 was the true scale for HO, early models from all these makers tended to have overscale

ABOVE:
Progress in the realistic representation of locomotives in miniature is well shown here where two tinplate O gauge ATSF (Santa Fe) F units in the famous 'warbonnet' livery, dating from the 1940s, flank the later plastic-bodied model of the 1960s from the same manufacturer.

bodies to fit the larger mechanisms of those days. Early Märklin HO models (both prewar and postwar) were mostly to 1:85 scale, while Fleischmann and others tended to use 1:82 scale. It is only in comparatively recent years (the 1980s) that the last of the old overscale models disappeared from production and everything in HO is now truly 1:87 scale.

One very major change that took place during the war years was the switch for two-rail HO from 6 volts to 12 volts. This was instigated in America by the NMRA and Al Kalmbach, and when postwar production resumed everyone adopted it as a world standard. Only a few AC systems remain (for example Märklin and Trix Express in Germany) which do not conform to this. Trix converted to two-rail 12 volt DC with a parallel range to the AC models which they call Trix International. The old Trix Twin concept was abandoned in the process. The main French maker in HO since the late 1950s has been Jouef, still very active, but there was also a very fine French range by Hornby-Dublo, known as Hornby-Acho, made by Meccano's French factory until the collapse in the 1960s. Another well-known French name was JEP who were mainly producing O gauge 'toy' models in France until the 1960s.

A significant newcomer in Europe was an Austrian engineer, Heinz Rössler, who

TOP:
These typical British toy models of the 1950s, in tinplate and powered by batteries are a Chad Valley Merlin (blue) 2-4-0 and a Mettoy 2-4-0.

ABOVE:
A Fleischmann 12 volt DC O gauge locomotive and luggage van from 1950.

RIGHT:
A selection of American Flyer die-cast and plastic S gauge, including (no. 88) an excellent model of the classic 'American' 4-4-0, the most common American locomotive a century or more ago.

founded a plastic toy molding company in 1960, called Roco. They started making military models in 1:87 scale from a factory at Salzburg. Sales in America led to a request from the American firm of AHM for freight car models in HO to the same high standard of molding. This in turn led to contract work for established German model railway companies. By 1967 Rössler decided to use his expertise to produce his own model railway range, with an initial release of Austrian and German freight stock. In 1973 the firm moved into making locomotives, too, and the first model, a Deutsche Bundesbahn Class 215 diesel loco set new standards for HO. Not only was it beautifully molded and finished, but it had flywheel drive, a can motor, and printed circuit 'wiring', etc, all more technically advanced than anything offered by rival firms. The model (still available in the 1990s) set a standard that Roco has kept to (and improved on) ever since, making it a major world producer of model trains. Roco soon overshadowed its rival Austrian firm, Liliput, founded in 1947, and this company was eventually taken over by Bachmann in 1992, moving production to Hong Kong in the process.

The German firm of Röwa, which flourished in Neckar in the 1960s, set new high standards in HO, and conceived the idea of a 'universal' coupler pocket which allowed close coupling of adjacent vehicles. In the early 1970s Röwa ceased trading, but many of their molds and ideas passed to Roco who pushed the 'universal' coupler idea well and for some years now it has been an European standard, used by all HO makers.

The 1960s, and the decades since, have seen a profusion of model railway development in Europe. Rivarossi started in Italy in the 1950s with some very pleasing HO models, initially of Italian types but soon branching out into excellent locomotives, mostly of the steam age, and rolling stock for the American market. Lima came along in the 1960s as a second force in Italy, eventually expanding to produce models for every country in Europe, including Britain, plus a few for the United States. Both companies also produced N gauge ranges and both also made ranges of O gauge ready-to-run models in plastic in the 1970s and 1980s which were in similar style to current HO models. Unfortunately O gauge did not catch on in Europe even at the reasonable prices of these models. For the modern O

gauge enthusiast, however, they are very desirable models.

Much the same thing happened in Germany. Pola-Maxi (later Railmo) made an excellent range of German O gauge models in plastic in the 1970s and 1980s, but, again, they failed to achieve mass market sales and were not continued. In Germany and other main European countries there is certainly a following for O gauge but it is met today by higher-priced, exquisitely detailed models made in very limited numbers (and sometimes in kit form) by such firms as Allgo and Lemaco (Switzerland), and Kiss, MicroMetakit, Wunder, and Bavarian Models (Germany). The specialist making individual models to order is at the very pinnacle of the hobby and

TOP:
Cheap American toy trains of the 1950s, with a Unique Lines caboose, a clockwork locomotive, and a gondola and box car by Hafner, all for O gauge.

ABOVE:
The new Märklin Maxi series in gauge 1, introduced in 1994. Finished in tinplate, the trains feature digitalized electric control and steam sound units.

ABOVE:
Some of the finest commercial models today come from the Austrian firm of Roco. Here is their superbly detailed HO model of the advanced Swiss Re 460 'new generation' electric locomotive in its original Swiss Federal Railways (SBB) form at the bottom, with a version for the Swiss Bern-Lötschberg-Simplon (BLS) line in the center (Class Re 465), and the export version of the same locomotive for Finland at the top.

their models are of high value to any collector rich enough to commission or acquire one. The doyen of all specialist builders was the late Stanley Beeson whose models grace museums and exclusive collections, each one a jewel of the model-making art. Bernard Miller was another British master modeler who was highly regarded, and today's master

modelers in Britain include Vic Green and Derek Lawrence.

In America the top end of the hobby is devoted to brass handmade models in all popular scales, made in limited runs by craftsmen in Japan and Korea. This notion had its origins in the aftermath of World War 2 when model enthusiasts serving with the occupying US Army discovered the intricate skill of Japanese craftsmen. This led to several firms in America importing the models and 'brass' became almost a sub-division of the hobby in its own right with models being purchased and traded for their investment value. This 'brass' interest continues, though the market, having been flooded, is much quieter today than it was in the 1950-70 period. Some brass models have been made for the British, European, and Australian markets and they still appear from time to time. Because of the limited batch production these beautiful brass models are rare and appreciate in value.

Perhaps because of the firm's marketing power, when Märklin launched a modern plastic gauge 1 range in the early 1970s, with fine scale models made to the highest standards, it fared much better than the O gauge ranges launched by others at the same time. Märklin gauge 1 still exists, and a bold

RIGHT:
Early postwar Australian O gauge models, featuring a Maurlyn electric streamlined 4-6-2 with a Robilt bogie, breakdown crane and van.

and exciting move in the mid-1990s was the launch by Märklin of a new all-metal gauge 1 Maxi range, officially for children, but of undoubted appeal to all model rail enthusiasts who like substantial, good-looking models. The Maxi range will obviously be tomorrow's collectors' pieces. The Maxi models are a far cry from the Märklin tinplate models of old, though they have a similar character. The mechanisms and chassis are right up to date, justifying Märklin's slogan 'Playing trains with today's technology.' Gauge 1 in Germany is also catered for by several specialist firms who support Märklin's mass market effort, among them, Hübner and Kessellbauer.

Swinging from one extreme to the other, Märklin used the dynamic growth period of the 1970s to launch another new gauge, this time called Z, with a scale of 1:220 and a track gauge of 6.5mm. This flourishes almost entirely thanks to Märklin, the only other big manufacturer in Z being Micro-Trains Line in America, who are also a leading N gauge maker and the producer of excellent magnetic couplers in these small scales. For HO and larger scales Micro-Trains' associate company, Kadee, makes the magnetic coupler system, devised in the 1950s by Keith and Dale Edwards (hence 'Kadee') and which is unsurpassed by any other in miniature form.

The European modeler is also well served by TT, 1:120 scale, 2.5mm to one foot, which has been produced in Germany by Berliner-Bahn and others since the 1950s.

Today, in fact, the keen model railway enthusiast is spoilt for choice. The spread of interests covered is almost too good to be true. For example, if you are attracted by the idea of a layout in the style of prewar tinplate O gauge, the Spanish firm of Paya still make models from this era and have a range with a good following for those who enjoy the charm of printed tinplate. Paya have distributors in most countries, including Britain and Germany. The Czech firm of ETS also make modern tinplate. If you want the magnificence of live steam in gauge 1, the Swiss firm of Fulgurex, in conjunction with the Japanese firm of Aster, supplies beautiful limited run models of great perfection (and high price) with new subjects every year which instantly become sought-after pieces. Among numerous models released in recent years are the classic Great Western *King George V*, an American Shay geared loco, and a huge Australian Beyer-Garratt articulated steamer.

On the other hand if your disposable income is more modest you could do much worse than collect any of the good HO models of today, such as those by Roco, Athearn, Kato, Trix, Märklin, Fleischmann, and the others. While they may not seem all that significant when you acquire them, most have some sort of rarity value in as little as ten years time. For example, anyone who had purchased early cheap and cheerful Triang OO or TT models in, say, 1960, now has a most valuable and interesting asset which shows the sort of trains and color schemes encountered in Britain at that time.

CHAPTER FIVE
Collecting Today

BELOW:
Classic tinplate models of the 1930s. A Great Western O gauge layout using only Hornby models and equipment; the steel track is modern but in the style of the original Hornby track. The nearest locomotive is County of Bedford, *one of the most sought-after Hornby models.*

It is easy enough to make a start in model railway collecting: every model or hobby store has a big selection of tempting kits and models, but each enthusiast will have different interests and ideas on what constitutes a collection. You can, in fact, tailor the hobby to suit your precise situation, taking into account the money, time and space available. These factors will probably influence which scale or scales of models you will collect and particular railway interests and model-making skills should also be considered.

There are models to suit every pocket, and a collection can be built up gradually, as and when you can afford it, and spread over many years if necessary. Space or lack of it could well affect your approach. If you live in a small apartment, or are a student, or a traveler, you won't have room for a big collection of gauge

O or gauge 1 models. On the other hand, a collection of 50 or more N or Z gauge models would fit easily inside a shoebox. Time is clearly significant. If you are retired or have a lot of leisure, then you may be happy with a collecting subject like trams or trolley cars, where most models come in kit form and demand a lot of constructional work. Busier people might go for the ready-to-run trains in popular scales which are widely stocked and need little work for display or operation. Special interests will clearly influence the course of the hobby. If you are intrigued by the history of the model railway hobby, for example, you might be happy just to seek out any old models or literature in any scale. Fans of a particular railway company may collect the appropriate models regardless of scale, or may insist on everything being in one particu-

LEFT:
A rare model for collectors. This is a gauge O live steam locomotive with simple oscillating cylinders by Bar-Knight, complete with its original instruction sheet.

BELOW:
One of the most popular Märklin gauge 1 clockwork trains, produced for sale in Great Britain in 1905. The locomotive is in Midland Railway colors. The four-wheel coach has lost its roof.

lar scale from one specific maker at one specific period, or any variation of these.

A collector may be interested in the Great Western Railway, for which many models have been produced in OO gauge. A collection of GWR models amassed over the past 20 years would be extensive, a veritable museum in miniature, showing the history of steam traction as it affected one company. Starting with the Dean single-wheeler and the Dean Goods of the 1890s, the early Churchward Prairies and Moguls of the 1900s, the various 4-4-0 and 4-6-0 classes, via the 'Castles' and 'Kings,' and finally including the modified 'Halls' of the postwar years; would provide a complete steam line-up. One could continue into the BR era with the distinctive Western Region diesel-hydraulic locomotives, finishing with the BR diesel engines like *Sir Edward Elgar* (Class 50) and *Isambard Kingdom Brunel* (Class 47), which were finished in commemorative Great Western style in the 1980s. This collection would only feature locomotives. Add to it matching coaches and freight vehicles and even the GWR road vehicles, and the result would be an admirable collection.

The GWR theme is just an example, but the basic idea can be applied to whatever region, period or scale the collector is interested in. A few similar themes might include Bavarian State Railways, Deutsche Reichsbahn 1920-49, Deutsche Bundesbahn 1949-present, any of the British 'Big Four' companies, any large American company such as Baltimore and Ohio, Santa Fe, Burlington Northern or Southern Pacific – the list is long and the permutations endless. Those listed have one thing in common: they are all popular, well-known companies for which many models and kits have been produced. A collector of average skills and income would be sensible to stick to one of these better-known themes, simply because there is plenty to collect, as well as a great deal of reference material for research and further inspiration. A more obscure theme, such as Norwegian Railways, for example, would be harder, but not impossible to collect. The same applies to some of the old British lines. Very few actual models have ever been produced in the popular ranges of trains from any of the small regional lines which existed prior to the 1923 railway grouping, and even the selection of kits is small, so building up a representative collection is not straightforward. An enthusiast of a more obscure era or line would have to build the few kits available and scratch-build the rest, so modeling skill and an ability to cope with quite complicated metal kits would be an additional asset. The alternative is to commission the building and painting of such models, although this is not a cheap option.

Many modelers, however, have built up beautiful collections on rarer themes, such as the North Staffordshire Railway, the London North Western Railway and the early railways of the 1840s. Virtually all the models in these collections have been handmade and painted; very few models in these categories can be purchased off the shelf, and even kits are

BELOW:
A superb example of scratch-building by Ken Thomas, who made and painted this LMS 4-4-0 Midland Compound.

scarce. A skilled modeler willing to devote time to a rare or obscure collection will undoubtedly find it immensely satisfying.

Historical collecting themes can be more rarified than anything so far mentioned. One of the most noted modelers active in the 1950s and 1960s collected and made only model signals, all in the most exquisite detail and completely authentic: he was a scholar on the subject. He was certainly a model railway collector even though a collection devoted only to signals would surprise many new to the hobby. Others have collected catalogs, brochures and showcards from model railway manufacturers, or the various cartons in which the models were sold. Some have collected only model road vehicles operated by railway companies, and others have concentrated on signal boxes or other structures. All of this is entirely valid, for railway infrastructure has a history of development just as surely as the trains themselves. Here we can see another great value in the model railway hobby as a whole, for the real railways are continually changing, and the old is swept away and disappears. But it lives on in miniature, whether in a locomotive, coach, signal, or building, so that everyone can see what it all

LEFT:
A craftsman hand-painting gauge 1 models at the Bassett-Lowke factory in the 1960s.

BELOW:
A ready-to-run commercial model enhanced with added details. This Hornby third-class Pullman Kitchen Car has detail added from Comet and MJT parts. Adding extra detail to small-scale models, or converting them to other variants, is a popular part of the hobby.

ABOVE:
An HO gauge model of the Norwegian (NSB) DI 3 class locomotive by Norsk Modell Jernbane. This is basically a Märklin model with the extra details and fittings carried on Norwegian locomotives of this type. The original is a Nohab design.

RIGHT:
A gauge 1 pre-1914 Bassett-Lowke Midland Railway tinplate brake van with its original box, and a complete set of Bassett-Lowke miniature tinplate advertisements for the same scale with their original packing. The brake van was originally in the personal collection of W. J. Bassett-Lowke, founder of the famous company.

LEFT:
Almost anything connected with model railways can be collected, and in time acquires historic interest. This even applies to seemingly mundane items such as power units. Here are four, old and new, spanning the period 1950-80, and showing considerable variation in style.

once looked like. Relatively few have seen Stephenson's celebrated *Rocket* locomotive of 1829 (which is preserved in its different final form at the Science Museum, London), but everyone who has seen a model of *Rocket* can instantly appreciate its significance. Collecting model railways, in short, has not only kept alive the heritage of model manufacturing, but it has also done its bit in preserving an awareness of railway history, each personal collection in effect being a small railway museum.

Not everyone is interested in historical themes. Over the years the leading companies that have supplied the model railway trade have themselves become famous for their output. The great names include Märklin, Trix, Bing, Fleischmann (Germany), Ives, Lionel, Mantua (USA), JEP, Jouef (France), Hornby, Bassett-Lowke, British Trix, Leeds, Graham Farish and Tri-ang (Great Britain). This has led to great brand loyalty among modelers, and over the years several clubs and societies have been formed especially for those whose major interest is in collecting the output of these companies. Thus, there are societies devoted to Märklin, Fleischmann, Trix, Hornby O gauge, Hornby-Dublo, Bassett-Lowke, Lionel, Tri-ang, and others. You can see the

fascination for collecting specific makes of models when you realize that Märklin has been making model trains for over 100 years, Hornby O gauge was in production for over 40 years, Fleischmann has been producing for about 45 years, and so on. With new models and revisions each year, the scope for collecting all the different models and variations is enormous. These days the companies themselves have added to the collecting craze by producing limited-run or one-run models, sometimes with numbered certificates and in presentation boxes, which instantly acquire rarity value as they will never be repeated. The assiduous collector of a specific make goes one better than this, often identifying variations (such as a minor color change or a trademark revision) that even the original maker did not record! Sometimes the packaging or box changed during a production run, and this is also of interest to a collector of the range. Sometimes there are unexpected rarities, the present Hornby company, for example, produced a fine model of British Rail's high-speed Advanced Passenger (tilt) Train in 1980 while the prototype train was being built. This was to be the flagship of the BR fleet, but unfortunately the train did not

not meet expectations and was canceled. Hornby, meanwhile, had produced the model, which it subsequently withdrew, since the real thing no longer ran on British Rail. The Hornby APT, therefore, has become one of the great rarities, with a value several times its original selling price.

The specialist societies catering for different makes are continually researching past models as well as catering for those who prefer the current ranges. They all produce newsletters or magazines for members and, in addition, several publishers have produced books covering past models from the ranges. These are invaluable, of course, for anyone new to the hobby who wants to know what to look for and get some idea of the scope. Of all the major makers it is probably Märklin who has the greatest number of enthusiasts worldwide, dedicated to buying and running their models and no others.

Types of Collection

As we have already seen, the scope of model railways is very wide indeed, and apart from the enormous subject area there are many scales and gauges. Within the hobby itself

TOP:
Typical accessories well worth collecting are road vehicles associated with rail traffic.

ABOVE:
A recent modern HO model of the German ICE train (Inter City Express) by Fleischmann, with a modern ICE train station platform from a kit by Vollmer.

RIGHT:
A gauge O clockwork Leeds Model Company Caledonian Railway 'Jumbo' 0-6-0 goods locomotive in LMS livery with a 1930s LMC catalog.

LEFT:
A small German goods yard layout in HO gauge, built by the author, which brings together a representative collection of modern German freight, rolling stock, and locomotives. The models shown here are by Roco, the locomotive being a DB Class 365.

BELOW:
The dramatic way to show off a large model railway collection is in custom-built showcases. This impressive display features British, American, and European models in HO and OO scales.

there are divisions of interest and specialization that of necessity restrict the average enthusiast to just one part of them, though there are plenty of keen hobbyists who get involved in more than one segment. The breadth of the model railway hobby is one of its strengths, because anyone interested in the idea of model trains is bound to find at least one area of special appeal.

Among the hobbyists themselves there are few who would care to define the term 'collecting model railways.' Even this expression means different things to different enthusiasts. A conventional viewpoint would take a model railway collection to mean well-ordered display cases with rows of gleaming miniature locomotives and trains nicely illuminated and annotated. Everything would be pristine and in original condition. Such collections certainly exist (and examples are illustrated), but in practice this sort of ornate presentation is not all that common. Many more enthusiasts have similar collections which spend much of the time in boxes and securely locked in cupboards, as much for

reasons of security as for storage if the models are of high value. At best these collectors may have the odd wall-mounted display case or a few shelves on which some of the more attractive models are displayed, but even this is not common. It is more likely that the whole lot would be kept stored away. If space is short this may be the only option in any case, but it does not invalidate the interest of the collection.

There is another huge group of model railway enthusiasts who would consider it anathematic to own interesting model trains and then keep them locked away in cupboards and showcases, never turning a wheel or running along track. These are the active modelers who build layouts on which the model locomotives and rolling stock actually run under realistic conditions. They are regarded as working models and they operate in miniature surroundings. Usually the models are all closely related, accurately detailed and painted, and as close to the real thing as it is possible to get. These enthusiasts would call themselves 'modelers' rather than 'collectors,' and might not even consider their

BELOW:
The most sought-after and valuable of all the Hornby O gauge range is the magnificent Princess Elizabeth *of the late 1930s, seen here in its original wooden box with instruction booklet.*

ABOVE:
The most widely sold and produced of all HO Japanese-made brass models in the 1960s and early 1970s was the little Porter Mogul 2-6-0 by Ken Kidder, a good model of a small American branch-line locomotive.

models to be a collection. Another group of modelers favor large-scale models, often with live steam locomotives, running on tracks in the garden – true engineering in miniature – and they would probably consider themselves to be 'model engineers' rather than 'collectors.' But, in truth, all these enthusiasts are model railway collectors the moment they start acquiring models, and how they use them after that is rather incidental. As there are no rules and regulation in the model railway hobby, you can do whatever appeals to you most. There are some who prefer to keep new models gleaming and in factory finish if they are of famous makes; others who can afford to have models made to order, or prefer to make exotic models from kits; and yet others who prefer to add all the tiny details that a mass-production model might lack, then add the dirt and grime of a working locomotive. Some will take pride in displaying their models in showcases, while others have the ambition to build a highly detailed layout with all the trains operating.

Even models in the latter category constitute interesting collections. For example, noted British modeler Richard Gardner has a fine layout called Stokenham which is seen at many model rail exhibitions. Richard would not describe himself as primarily a collector, but the many locomotives and trains running on the Stokenham layout together make up a superb collection of British Railways, Western Region, stock as it appeared around 1960 in South Devon, the setting and era of the layout. If the models were not hard at work on the layout they would look just as interesting if lined up in display cases to be admired at close quarters, even though all the locomotives have grimy working finishes and alterations which make them far removed from the original gleaming, freshly painted, mass-produced models from makers like Hornby and Bachmann, which they actually are.

There is a parting of the ways in attitude between those who regard themselves as 'pure' collectors and those who are active modelers. To a pure collector, the value of a model lies in its original appearance as it left the maker, and ideally the model would retain its original box and packing as part of the collection. Such a collector is horrified at the idea of taking such a model, altering it by adding extra details, gluing coal in the tender, adding smoke and weathering effects as on real trains, and making it a grimy representation of the real thing. The divergence of views on this has to be accepted, but it must be said that in the collectors' market, where models are bought and sold secondhand, the high and

LEFT:
Action on a modern scenic HO layout, the Kahoka Falls & Western Railway.

RIGHT:
Atlas American O gauge models of the 1970s and 1980s running on a garden layout. The locomotive is a EMD F9 'covered wagon' in ATSF (Santa Fe) finish.

BELOW:
Owlcombe is a charming Great Western branch-line layout. The locomotive is a modified GWR pannier tank, made by Gaiety in the 1950s and quite rare today.

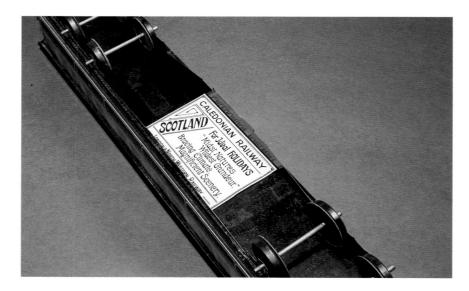

ABOVE:
Underside of one of the promotional Caledonian Railway coaches made for Bassett-Lowke by Carette in 1909-10 showing the Caledonian advertisement affixed under each coach.

the story behind the model. Building a layout may have no appeal at all for this enthusiast, but because of the broad nature of the hobby any attitude is valid. In fact, there is much to be said for these different approaches. Working layouts are fascinating, whether built yourself or seen at exhibitions, but if there were not a considerable number of enthusiasts carefully collecting, conserving, and even trading mint-condition railway models over many years we would not be able to enjoy the rich model railway heritage that there is today.

It is possible to take both approaches simultaneously if there are particular models that appeal to you as an active model layout builder. For example, Hornby (and their predecessor company Tri-ang) has long offered a very attractive OO gauge model of the celebrated Bulleid streamlined *West Country/Battle of Britain* Light Pacific. Over the years it has appeared in various liveries and names. The model has great intrinsic charm as purchased, and looks good in its box. But for the purist it has a number of detail errors and omissions and certainly does not look like a hard-working, slightly grimy 'hack,' as most of them were. The answer is to buy two models (as the author did). One is kept pristine in its box as a genuine collectors' piece, while the other is much reworked and has incorrect detail replaced, extra detail added, coal glued in the tender top, crew figures added in the cab, and a grimy working finish. This is the model used on a layout. Its second-

appreciating value remains with the unaltered model in its original box. The same model with added details, lots of weathering, and without its box will have a very low secondhand value. How you approach this depends entirely on your point of view and the pleasure you want to derive from the hobby. Some are never happier than when building working layouts, and they may have no great ambition ever to trade the models, merely regarding them as raw material for model-making fun. Others have a genuine regard for model manufacturing history, and would not want to alter a model from the gleaming condition in which they bought it. They may have no modeling skill anyway, and may be very happy swapping, bartering, and researching

RIGHT:
A plastic-bodied inexpensive clockwork toy train set in S gauge produced in East Germany in the 1980s. The track is also plastic.

hand value won't be much, but the model kept in its original box, just as it was purchased, increases in sale value by the year.

All collections need to be well maintained, and if they are particularly valuable, it is sensible to keep them somewhere secure. Wall-mounted showcases are useful: many are designed to hold complete trains, they look good, and protect their contents from dust. Original boxes and packing should, ideally, be kept in closets away from exposure to light.

Wheels and mechanisms should be kept clean and well lubricated, even if the models are rarely used on layouts. Spare parts can be obtained from larger model and hobby shops, or manufacturers. Extreme care should be taken with older models; clumsy repainting can ruin a rare piece which may retain its charm and value better in a worn state. There are specialists who offer an expert restoration service for tinplate models, for example.

There are no rules about acquiring models. Quite obviously current models are obtainable from hobby stores and mail-order specialists. Many big hobby stores also have secondhand departments. There are also traders who specialize in tinplate, old Hornby, Bassett-Lowke, and other famous brands. There are many 'swapmeets,' sometimes called 'toy train meets' or 'toy train shows,' where old model trains (and more recent ones) are exclusively traded. Typically these take place at weekends and are advertised locally, sometimes they are genuine swapmeets, where individuals can barter, but very often they provide stalls for specialist traders. Some antique and 'toy collector' shows, held in similar circumstances, also include toy trains among the items traded. Some antique shops have toy trains from time to time, and very occasionally you still meet someone who has just found an old train set in the attic or basement.

There are several advertising papers in which old model trains may be advertised. Some toy collector journals have similar adverts, and many of the model railway magazines include personal sales and wants adverts for old models, as well as giving news of all the swapmeets taking place that month. So it is a good idea to get some model railway magazines, at least one a month if you can afford it. The magazines also carry news of new products and lots of inspiring articles and background information to aid your hobby. News and announcements of clubs and the specialist collecting societies are also carried in all the model railway journals. Finally, visit any local model railway shows. These will not only give you inspiration, but there are often bargains to be found.

ABOVE:
Preussen Gloria! *The
Prussian royal train,
Imperial court, Guards*

*band, and the Kaiser's
limousine, as made by
Märklin in O gauge in
1909.*

Appendices

Model Railway Journals

Model railway magazines are always required reading for model railway collectors and builders. Apart from the informative material and news they carry, they also give information on products, sales, swapmeets, flea markets, mall shows, and other venues, such as model railway exhibitions, where models new or old can be acquired. The following list is of major publications.

United States
Model Railroader
Railroad Model Craftsman
Railroad Journal

Great Britain
Scale Model Trains
Railway Modeller
Model Railway Enthusiast
Model Railways Illustrated
British Railway Modelling

Germany
Eisenbahn Illustrierte
Modell Eisenbahn
Eisenbahn Journal
Eisenbahn Kurier
MIBA

France
Loco Revue
Rail Miniature Flash
Le Train

Further Reading

There are numerous books covering collecting, quite apart from titles on railway modeling and constructing in general. Some publications give highly-detailed coverage of specific ranges from the past and are of obvious value to anyone specializing in those ranges.

New titles appear all the time and others go out of print. Larger transport specialist bookshops and the bigger model shops usually stock a collection. For the British modeler the large series published by New Cavendish is of particular interest. The following titles are just a small selection:

Harley-Dublo Compendium, A. T. Ellis

The Hornby Gauge O System/Hornby Gauge O Compendium, C. Graebe
Hornby-Dublo Trains, 1938-64, M. Foster
The Bassett-Lowke Story, R. Fuller
Toy Trains, D. Salisbury
Tri-ang Railways, Vol. 1, P. Hammond
Greenburg's Guides (At least ten volumes covering Lionel, American Flyer, Athearn, and other early US makers)
A. C. Gilbert's Heritage, D. Heimburger
American Flyer Features, D. Heimburger
American Toy Trains, Collector's Guide, S. Bagdade
Kolls Katalogs, Several volumes and editions covering Märklin output at various times
Märklin: The Golden Twenties, C. Baecker (And many other books by the same author covering Märklin history in great detail.)
Walters Katalog, K. E. Hennig (Several volumes covering Märklin over the years)
Sammlerkatalog, R. Schiffmann (Five volumes covering early Bing and Märklin models)
Bing Modellbahnen, C. Jeanmaire

In addition there are several catalog reprints available, including Bing for 1906 and 1926, while several Meccano/Hornby catalogs and Lionel catalogs, etc, have been reprinted in facsimile at various times.

Clubs and Societies

The following clubs and societies are of special interest to collectors, and in most cases they produce regular news letters or magazines. For current addresses and membership details see latest issues of model railway magazines.

Hornby Railway Collectors' Association
TTR Collectors' Association (Trix-Twin)
Italian Railway Society
Scandanavian Railway Society
SNCF Society (French)
German Railway Society
Gauge O Guild
S Gauge Model Railway Society
Gauge 1 Model Railway Association
Fleischmann Model Railway Club
3mm Society
Märklin Model Club (UK, German, and US branches)
N Gauge Society
Lionel Collectors' Club of America

Acknowledgments

Editor: Judith Millidge
Picture Researcher: Suzanne O'Farrell
Designer: Ron Callow of Design 23
Production: Simon Shelmerdine

We are grateful to the following for their generosity in making their collections available to us: the Reverend Alan Cliff, Mike Dawkins, the Peter and Joan Dunk Collection, Richard Gardner, Chris Lewis and Bert Pollard, Ian Rathbone, Tennent's Small Trains, and Ned Williams. In addition, David Brown, the editor of *British Railway Modelling* magazine, provided invaluable advice, and photographers Tony Wright and Nick Nicholson tracked down a number of perfectly-preserved models.

We would like to thank the following individuals and institutions for permission to reproduce the photographs on the pages noted below:

Wolfgang Berendt 6, 23 (top), 24, 30-31, 33 (top), 78

Bristol Museum and Art Gallery 52 (below), 55 (top)

Chris Ellis 7 (below), 10 (top), 12 (below), 14, 39, 41, (all 3), 50 (both), 51 (top), 62 (top), 66, 68 (top), 70 (top 2), 71 (top), 73, 75 (both)

Märklin 17 (top), 61 (below)

Brian Monaghan 7 (top), 8, 10 (below), 11, 12 (top), 67 (top), 71 (below) 74

Andrew Morland 1, 27, 43 (top)

Nick Nicholson Photography 3, 13, 21 (both)

The Science Museum, London 18, 19, 20

Sotheby's 22 (below)

Tony Wright Photography 4-5, 9, 16, 17 (below), 22, 25, 26, 28, 29, 32 (both), 34, 35, 36, 37 (both), 38, 40, 42 (both), 43 (below) 44, 45, 46 (both), 47, 48 (both), 49, 51 (below), 52 (top). 53, 54, 55 (below), 56, 57 (both), 58, 59, 60 (all 3), 61 (top), 62 (below), 63, 64, 65 (both), 67 (below), 68 (below), 69, 70 (bottom), 72